sex *with*
your
ex...

and 69 other things you should never do again

...plus a few that you should

Yvonne K. Fulbright, Ph.D.

A LARK PRODUCTION

PoLKA DoT
press

Adams Media
Avon, Massachuse

D1019916

The Polka Dot Press® name and logo design
are registered trademarks of F+W Publications, Inc.

Published by
Adams Media, an F+W Publications Company
57 Littlefield Street, Avon, MA 02322. U.S.A.
www.adamsmedia.com

ISBN-10: 1-59869-205-4
ISBN-13: 978-1-59869-205-1

Printed in the United States of America.

J I H G F E D C B A

Library of Congress Cataloging-in-Publication Data
is available from publisher.

This publication is designed to provide accurate and authoritative information with regard to the subject matter covered. It is sold with the understanding that the publisher is not engaged in rendering legal, accounting, or other professional advice. If legal advice or other expert assistance is required, the services of a competent professional person should be sought.
—From a *Declaration of Principles* jointly adopted by a Committee of the American Bar Association and a Committee of Publishers and Associations

Many of the designations used by manufacturers and sellers to distinguish their product are claimed as trademarks. Where those designations appear in this book and Adams Media was aware of a trademark claim, the designations have been printed with initial capital letters.

*This book is available at quantity discounts for bulk purchases.
For information, please call 1-800-289-0963.*

This book is dedicated to
Rick, Mark, Luke, Cowen, Tae, Wett, Albert, and Gog
For being the best friends a girl could ever have.

Contents

Introduction

As a sexologist and relationship expert, I have always endorsed a permission-giving approach when it comes to educating people about intimacy and sexual wants. In a society full of negative messaging about sexuality, I've tried to help people feel positive about their sexuality and their sexual desires and to dispel notions that sex is taboo, dirty, or wrong. I encourage people to figure out what's best for them and their partners when it comes to sexual decision-making—and not just accept what has been dictated to them by society or our media culture.

So why would I want to write a bossy little book telling people what never to do? Because the word "never" catches your attention—and even though I know you're going to do what you want to do (with or without my advice), these eyebrow-raising "nevers" may just keep you connected to your own good sense when it comes to sex, relationships, and other interpersonal behavior. Sometimes we learn from our own mistakes; sometimes we learn from others' mistakes. This book is a reflection of the common (and occasionally uncommon!) experience of all kinds of people just like you. They fall in love, they fall in lust, they hook up, they break up, they struggle to make sense of the situations in which they find themselves. We all recognize the horror and the humor in some of those situations, remembering all too well the regrettable things that can happen by our own choices. The good news is that every day offers a new beginning in making better choices, every relationship an opportunity to have a happy ending, every sexual encounter a chance to be safe and have the time of your life. So if you are sheepishly reminded of some of your own mistakes in these 70 nevers, take heart in the fact that you have your whole life ahead of you to get it right—and have a blast doing it!

I hope you have fun with this book, the way you would with a good friend who knows you well and you can always have a laugh with. You know, the kind of friend who's good at gently pointing out to you when you're headed down an unfortunate path or who helps you get back on your feet when things go wrong. This is the best kind of friend to have, and the pages of this book are full of them—people who generously shared the benefit of their own experience, no matter how mortifying it might have been. Thanks to all of them, and best of luck to you. Oh, and one last never: never forget to take care of yourself and those you care about. If you just do that, you're probably covered on the other 70 nevers in this book!

#1 ... Never have sex with your ex.

There's a long list of rock-solid reasons never to have sex with your ex, starting with whatever the reason your ex is your ex and not still your partner. But whether it's a chance encounter or an idea that's been rolling around in your brain for a while, the opportunity to have sex with your ex can be irresistible. Even if he wasn't the best lover you ever had, whatever burned between you in your prime time can start to seem pretty compelling, especially if you're rebounding from another relationship, not thinking clearly thanks to that third cocktail, or you just plain haven't had it for a while. In the heat of that kind of moment, it can seem like the *only* thing to do!

And you may as well forget it if he *was* the best lover you ever had. Especially if he's the one you still daydream about, the one you picture when taking your needs, ahem, into your own hands, the one who still makes your heart stop when you

I Can't Believe I Did That! I hadn't seen my ex in more than a decade when he called me out of the blue to say he was in town on business, and did I want to get together for a drink? Sure, why not? I thought. I'm just meeting a friend for a drink, I said to my current boyfriend, but then I found myself putting on the silk underwear and expensive scent as I got dressed for our rendezvous. Sure enough, one glass of wine and we were headed for his hotel room. The sex was great, but it only took one minute to remember why I broke up with him in the first place—I had hardly finished moaning when he flicked on ESPN to check Final Four scores. I went home to my sweet, considerate boyfriend and thanked my lucky stars.—Anne

remember how he took you to otherworldly places you haven't visited since. The prospect of a postscript tryst with *this* ex is *really* hard to resist.

The hard fact is that having sex with your ex-boyfriend, ex-husband, ex-partner, ex-one-night-stand, ex-whatever is playing with fire on too many levels for it ever to be the truly right thing to do. Strong feelings will resurface. You may long for him in ways that will surprise you. You may have to fight an overpowering lust. Powerful sex-triggered hormones in your body can make you think you're falling in love again. You will have amnesia about the reasons you're no longer together and be sucked into a fantasy of "happily ever after" this time. You will be tempted to think only of the good times, and you may even find yourself thinking about what could have been, what might still be . . . stop that!

There is a reason—probably several!—that this person is your ex, even if he broke up with you. And having sex will make you forget those reasons. Physical intimacy will bring back feelings you think you've buried, which might confuse you and cause you to make decisions you will later regret. Even if you think you're strong enough and removed enough from the past to have some nice sex and leave it at that, the hurts, the longings, the issues, and the drama will likely replay in your mind long beyond your short burst of passion.

The question to ask yourself is this: will you be able to get on with your life if this little roll turns out to be no more than a love affair's final curtain call? Can you truly close the door—again—or are you opening Pandora's box? If you harbor even the slightest whiff of a fantasy that going to bed with your ex is going to rekindle your relationship, heal all its wounds, right all its wrongs—run, don't walk in the other direction. Sex with your ex can't do that. Unless he's been doing some major work on himself and his issues, he's likely the same person he was when you broke up.

How to say "no" to sex with your ex

- Make a list of reasons why you broke up in the first place. If his being a selfish or bad lover is on the list, why even bother? You're not that desperate!
- Ask yourself how you'll really feel in the morning. If you think this experience will be emotionally painful in any way, don't do it.
- Ask yourself whether you think your motives are only physical. Do you think *his* motives are only physical?
- Be firm and expect your rejection to cause your ex to want you even more.

Never have sex with your ex UNLESS . . .

- You had a pleasant, uncomplicated relationship and your breakup was amicable and mutually desired.
- You genuinely have unfinished business, perhaps having broken up over issues out of your control, still miss each other, and/or both think there's still something there. Oh, and neither of you is involved with anyone else!
- Years have passed, there's a safe, genial distance between you, and sex with someone familiar is just what the doctor ordered.

- You really are just friends now, and there's a mutual understanding that it's about sexual gratification, not emotional, and that there are no expectations beyond this moment.
- You use protection. Because you really *shouldn't* be having sex with your ex, you are going to have enough head-spinning post-ex-sex drama to sort through without coming away with a "souvenir."
- He can somehow prove that he's dealt with his issues.
- You're as much of a narcissist as he turned out to be—you're made for each other!
- He's no longer your ex!

#2 ... Never have sex with a friend simply for the benefits.

Having a "friend with benefits" sounds so . . . friendly! What you really have, though, is a relationship known as a "booty call," and while convenient and often pleasant, it's a much more complicated and potentially hazardous arrangement than it seems. With no maintenance, no commitment, little time investment, and the potential to gratify sexual, animal urges, booty calls appeal to a number of adults who are too busy, too burned out, or too bummed about love to pursue more traditional, demanding relationships. Simple desire, sexual experimentation, physical pleasure, and alcohol use are also among the reasons many men and women cite for engaging in this particular sort of laissez-faire sexual liaison.

While men and women participate in booty-call relationships for the same basic reasons, their different underlying attitudes toward casual sex can introduce an element of conflict

and negative drama, especially over time. Research continuously confirms that men have more genuinely permissive attitudes toward casual sex than do women, despite what modern, sexually "liberated" women would have you believe. Furthermore, men tend to have casual sex for social-environmental reasons, like status enhancement or peer pressure, whereas women are likelier to have it for interpersonal reasons, such as increasing the probability of a sex partner committing for the long term. (In other words, a guy might be able to keep his side of a booty-call gig strictly casual, but a woman may find herself making more of it, even unconsciously.)

Booty-call relationships can give two people who are comfortable with each other the opportunity to explore an array of sexual experiences. Yet having casual, physical intimacy—even with someone you know well—still calls for careful consideration no matter how free of land mines it may appear at first. What might seem like utopia at the time may not be so wise in retrospect. Partners can have different expectations, emotions can unexpectedly come into play, and any disrespect can turn into trouble—and harm your friendship or ruin it altogether.

No matter how solid you think your friendship is and how separate you think you can keep the sex from the mechanics of your friendship, something eventually comes up that makes you say, "Hmm, this doesn't seem like such a good idea any more." Or, worse yet, you may start thinking, "Maybe I do dig him for more than his hip action." That's because friendship is a living, breathing thing, with the same emotional hues that color any other relationship. Having sex together isn't like sharing popcorn at a movie—sex is inherently intimate and *will* bump up against your friendship at some point.

I Can't Believe I Did That! Having always thought my friend Isaac was cute, and feeling terribly lonely in the big city, I found myself regularly hanging out with him, becoming more and more intimate each time—snuggling on the couch over our favorite TV shows, kissing during commercial breaks, trading oral pleasures after David Letterman. I warned him that my heart wasn't in it, but he was a warm body and helped me to not feel so lonely. The only rule we had was to tell the other if we became intimate with somebody else; neither of us really thought we wanted anything more. And it didn't seem like a bad deal at the time, but eventually I came to understand why it sucked. Even though my heart wasn't involved, Isaac ended up breaking it anyway. When he went home for Christmas, he slept with his ex-girlfriend from high school, which he told me about right away. I was so insulted, despite our rules, that I quit sleeping with him. And sadly enough, our friendship was over, too.—Marcy

Bottom line: If you truly care about your friendship, don't monkey it up with sex. And if your friendship isn't really much of a friendship, you're really just having casual sex with someone you know and care about a little. That's another matter entirely.

Instead of fooling around with a friend . . .

- Masturbate.
- Have a different kind of bonding experience with your friend, like cow-tipping or rock climbing.
- Avoid those lonely-and-horny nights at home that make you call up your FWB in the first place. Get out and get a life!

#3 ... Never reveal your number of sexual partners.

This is an unequivocal never. Ever. That's because no matter what you tell your partner—that you've slept with two people, two hundred people, or no one but him—what happens to that information inside his brain is beyond your control. There is no upside to sharing this information . . . or asking it of your partner. Too many people fret and obsess over their partner's (or their own) sexual experience (or lack thereof). This may be because they are insecure or have moral or sexual-health concerns or believe that a person's ability to commit to a relationship is threatened by a heavily populated sexual past. Even if they don't have an issue with the score, they may worry what others think. Every guy wants sex with the good-time girl, but few would actually commit to her. Some people figure that if they know the number, then they can play psychic, predicting their partner's STD status and chance of being faithful. If you seem high-risk, they're not going to be interested in more than a one-time gamble. While it may not be honest, don't fess up your number unless proven guilty.

AND THAT'S A FACT: How come the words for a guy who has had many partners sound fun—like ladies' man, rake, or scoundrel—and the words for a sexually experienced woman are derogatory—slut, whore, or tramp? That's because society expects women to be sexually reserved, and calls women names when they break that convention. But it appears that this male-versus-female double standard may be evolving. Research involving college students has found no difference in participants' ratings of the acceptability of men and women's sexual behaviors—like heavy petting, sexual intercourse, and oral-genital contact—at various stages of a relationship. So women in this demographic are not receiving more negative reviews for having high numbers of past sexual partners in casual, noncommitted relationships. Furthermore, liberal men and women give more positive evaluations to women who are sexually experienced than to men of similar experience, and they find sexually experienced males to be less well-adjusted, less likable, and bad dating partners. Yet regardless of the gender, research shows that people feel that persons who engage in first intercourse in a noncommitted relationship or as a young teenager (versus young adulthood) are less desirable. They are considered less moral, less conventional, more assertive, more sexual, and less conforming. So, the good news is that we're all being (mis)judged the same way about our sexual history, regardless of gender!

It is understandable that lovers are curious and want to figure out what "kind" of lover is sharing their bed. Is this a promiscuous person or a goody two-shoes? But even more serious—and mistaken—assumptions are made based on this information. Sharing this number can trigger unwarranted judgment, jealousy, and speculation, mounting you on a sexual crucifix of sorts, making your partner think things about you that simply aren't true. So why bother sharing? With so many negative

I Can't Believe I Did That! While on spring break, I met a guy and slept with him within an hour of meeting him. I later asked him how many people he'd been with. He didn't want to tell me specifics, but he allowed that it was a lot. Terribly naive, and based on my own track record, I thought that a lot was like ten, fifteen partners, so I kept pressuring him for the tally. Finally, he told me that I was number thirty-three. My stomach dropped. I crawled out of bed, made my way to the bathroom, and puked. How could I have been so stupid to sleep with somebody so soon, and not knowing a thing about his sexual history? Thirty-three! He tried to tell me that that was his lucky number and that most of them had been virgins so that I had nothing to worry about disease-wise. Gee, that's comforting. I was planning to get tested for STDs after my vacation anyway, but knowing he had been so promiscuous only made me all the more nervous about the results! That was a tough lesson.—Shelley stereotypes and judgments potentially associated with one's sexual history, whether your number is "too few" or "too many," it's like playing the lottery—a scant few win. So keep your count in a safe for which only you know the combination.

Admittedly, when participating in a sensible, on-paper poll, most people claim they don't consider a potential partner's level of sexual experience to be as important as many other traits, such as dependable character, physical attractiveness, and ambition. But face to face, many potential loves-of-your-life are not carefully measuring that number against those important other qualities. People obsess about that number and what it might mean. Or rather, what they *think* it might mean! The simple rule is don't ask, don't tell. It's a can of worms that no one needs open. And there's something true and important to be said for maintaining an aura of mystery!

Instead of revealing your number of sexual partners . . .

- Lose your virginity all over again, doing something both of you have never done—in the sack or out!
- Tell him "Just enough." Then change the subject.
- Consider whether you want a partner who is going to place that much importance on your history and judge you on that alone.

#4 ... Never make out with someone while chewing gum.

No one wants to start making out with someone, hot on the trail of where all this kissing might lead, only to discover a wad of gum tucked under a partner's tongue. This is not sexy! You will have been totally busted in having primed for the action. And it's chewed-up gum he's playing with in your mouth, not your tasty tongue!

While gum advertisements would have you think that chewing their brand will make for the ultimate kiss, this candy doesn't always keep the action so fresh. Instead, it can become a distraction from the oral ecstasy you really long to savor, diverting your attention, creating uh-oh anxiety, and ultimately affecting your game. Ironically, that which made you once so minty-fresh and kissable can make the moment fizzle as the gum gets old, tasteless, and just plain in the way in your mouth—even causing bad breath!

I Can't Believe I Did That! I had met these two hot guys at a bar in the Village and decided to take them home with me, but not before offering them some gum first. As they chomped away, I had every woman's fantasy—I didn't have to do a thing as they took turns going down on me! It wasn't until the next morning that I realized that the gum hadn't been such a good idea after all. It was everywhere—all over my pubic hair! And all I could do was get out a pair of scissors and snip away. It seemed to take forever and it hurt—the gum had completely hardened. It was so gross. Funny, though, having never been that bare down there, I liked the results. I just wish I'd found out sans the gum.—Vivienne

And if you think Big League Chew can be bad at first base, wait until you get to third! You do not want gum anywhere near your genitals. In short, before you lock lips—anywhere— spit or swallow (and not the sexy way). Period.

#5 ... Never let him keep photos of you in your birthday suit.

No matter how you feel about newsstand porn, the thought of being the star of your very own birthday-suit shoot can be totally titillating. It's the perfect opportunity to dress up in your barely theres, show off your wares, and strike a pose. Plus, it's an opportunity to flirt with one cute photographer, especially if he helps you strip down to your tan lines!

Yet in capturing the thrilling moment, make sure that you, and only you, have access to these rare glimpses of you in your "finest" form. While your fantasy photo shoot can provide hours of entertainment, even breathing new life into future solo or joint sex sessions, be careful. While Mother Nature meant for you to be nude, society isn't in agreement with her on this one. And your actual mother might not like it too much either, should she stumble on your nudie pix on the Internet! That's

precisely where she'll find them if you don't keep them—each and every one of them—in your sole possession. Otherwise you can be sure your Pamela Anderson moment *will* come back to haunt you!

Another bit of advice: Don't make prints from digital photos or develop rolls of film. Besides the free thrill you'll be giving the film-developing guy at Wal-Mart, you introduce an

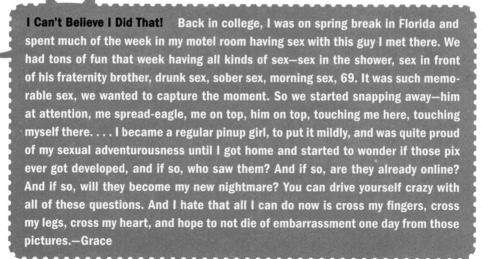

I Can't Believe I Did That! Back in college, I was on spring break in Florida and spent much of the week in my motel room having sex with this guy I met there. We had tons of fun that week having all kinds of sex—sex in the shower, sex in front of his fraternity brother, drunk sex, sober sex, morning sex, 69. It was such memorable sex, we wanted to capture the moment. So we started snapping away—him at attention, me spread-eagle, me on top, him on top, touching me here, touching myself there. . . . I became a regular pinup girl, to put it mildly, and was quite proud of my sexual adventurousness until I got home and started to wonder if those pix ever got developed, and if so, who saw them? And if so, are they already online? And if so, will they become my new nightmare? You can drive yourself crazy with all of these questions. And I hate that all I can do now is cross my fingers, cross my legs, cross my heart, and hope to not die of embarrassment one day from those pictures.—Grace unlimited photocopy-ability factor. One print is as good as a hundred—count on it. And don't ever e-mail a picture of your naked self, no matter how hot you want to make someone. A digital photo transmitted by e-mail will end up in the wrong hands—likely several million of them.

Best-case scenario: You have fun taking hot pix with your partner, preferably with your digital camera. You have more fun looking at those hot pix together. Then you delete those hot pix, no harm done. Or, if you must keep them so you can remember how hot you looked during the "prime" of your life, burn them onto a CD and put the CD in a safe-deposit box (making sure to also delete the pictures from the card after you've burned the CD). Don't even think about trying to disguise or hide this CD in your home—one day someone *will* find it. And you don't want that someone to be a future partner (who might not enjoy seeing pix of you going down on another guy), a future child (traumatized!), or the aforementioned mother.

Never let him keep pictures of you in your birthday suit UNLESS . . .

🔪 Your face isn't in the shot and there are no other identifiers in the picture, such as that one-of-a-kind tattoo you have.

- You're spending the rest of your lives together.
- You pose nude for a living, so this will in no way harm your career.
- You hope to pull a Paris Hilton–style rise to fame.

#6 ... Never let your friend sleep with somebody you have dirt on.

To tell or not to tell, that is the question. Sometimes what somebody doesn't know can't hurt them, right? But if you happen to know your friend's guy is cheating on her, has a shady history, or is simply up to no good, isn't it better to let her know? Honesty tends to be the best policy, but does it have to come from you? This quandary seems to have many facets and gray areas, but it really has only one good answer: Tell her.

Here's a good example of why. While at a dinner party, Raquel found out that her best friend's ex-boyfriend had been cheating on her during their entire two years together. She decided not to tell her friend, fearing that it would devastate her, even though the couple had already broken up amicably after he received orders to serve in Iraq. Raquel figured, since their breakup had nothing to do with the guy's philandering

and there was no reconciliation in sight, it ultimately didn't matter. So in her decision to protect her friend, Raquel also decided it was best for her friend to remember the relationship as something it truly was not. She stayed firm in her decision even when the ex unexpectedly returned from Iraq and started contacting her friend in hopes of getting back together. She stuck by her guns even when the guy suddenly ceased all contact with her friend upon learning, through the grapevine, that the hounds were onto his past wrongs and threatening to bust him if he didn't come clean. To this day, Raquel's friend doesn't know why the guy who promised to spend the rest of his life with her suddenly dropped her. So did Raquel do the right thing?

The "to tell or not to tell" dilemma is a classic damned if you do, damned if you don't scenario. But usually, you're more damned if you don't. Even a good friend has the tendency to shoot the messenger when it involves bad news. Either way, you could lose your friend—whether you tell her something she doesn't want to hear or she finds out from another source and realizes what you knew and didn't tell her. In deciding whether or not to dish the dirt, consider whether the information will help your friend more than it would hurt her to find out you knew and didn't tell. If the situation were reversed, would you want her to tell you? Could not telling her the scoop make things worse for her—for example, in this case, pining away for a cheater?

Most people who hear Raquel's situation feel that she should have told her friend. They were close and her friend deserved to know the truth, no matter how difficult to hear. Yet every such scenario is unique and you have to determine, without underestimating her strength, how well your friend can handle the news. On the other hand, withholding puts you in an inappropriate position of determining fate. Your deciding

AND THAT'S A FACT: Why is it that you can finally work up the nerve to tell a friend a bad bit of dirt about her guy and then she just goes on as if she never heard it? That's because advice is only helpful if the receiver is open to hearing it. Lots of times people don't want to hear upsetting news or information that will interfere with plans they have for themselves—such as living happily ever after with that louse you just busted to no avail. Be prepared for an angry reaction to this sort of bad news, and even straight-out denial. Sometimes people would rather put their hands over their ears and sing a happy song to themselves than face the unpleasant truth. Or they're willing to rag on their partner, but don't want to hear it if somebody else does, even if it's totally warranted. And there's nothing you can do about that.

what your friend should know or not know is a huge responsibility. And could you "handle" it if your decision backfired and ended up harming your friend in other ways?

Tell if it really matters and if it's true. Anything that falls in the category of insupportable gossip is just that—gossip. It doesn't deserve repeating to your friend or anyone else. But if you know something is true—say you've seen it, heard the dirt from people who are directly involved, and/or confronted the cad yourself—then it warrants your attention.

One last hard-and-fast rule to keep in mind when it comes to such scenarios is that if a friend's sexual health is at risk, then you must tell the truth. Even if the friendship sours as a result, you can rest assured that you did the right thing in trying to protect your friend's health. You can't be faulted for that.

Never let your friend sleep with someone you have dirt on UNLESS . . .

- You share the dirt either anonymously or upfront and you're sure she knows all the facts heading into it.
- You tell her the scenario as if it were true of another person and gauge her reaction. Ask her how she'd handle the "hypothetical" situation. If she reacts reasonably, maybe she can handle herself in the situation.

#7 ... Never accept a lame proposal.

A marriage proposal doesn't need to be an on-his-knees-in-front-of-the-whole-world performance. That's not every man's style and that's not what every woman wants. At the same time, there's something to be said about a lame attempt at popping the question. In short, it's just not cool. While a proposal is just a proposal and not a whole marriage, it can be a pretty good indication of what he has to offer in the romance and sensitivity department, and gives a taste of what's to come.

If you love and honor yourself, if you think that you're special, if you think that you deserve a thoughtful "Will you marry me?"—never accept a lame proposal. Don't be afraid to say "no." Don't be afraid to say "do over," especially if you really do want to spend the rest of your life with him. You deserve the best, whether his attempt is as simple as a picnic in the park or as glorious as a proposal at the top of the Eiffel Tower.

Corey knows a lame proposal when she hears one. She has been married twice, but was proposed to four times. Lance was the bumbling and unfortunate boyfriend who proposed after a night of heavy drinking toward the end of their senior year of college because he couldn't think of what else they should do after graduating. (Now that's showing initiative!) After burping, he rolled over, and with sour, bourbon-heavy breath, he asked her if she'd go for it. Not knowing what else to do with her life, she accepted.

The second proposal she received was two years into a fierce relationship with a difficult and passionate man who proposed in the middle of a heated argument. Feeling low from her divorce a year earlier, she accepted, only to find herself single again three months after a Vegas wedding.

The third proposal was from Corey's rebound relationship. Vince was blessedly relaxed and low-key, a real vacation after dating Frank Sinatra. He was so low-key, though, that one day he said, "I guess we probably ought to get married," as if he was suggesting they go out for a pizza. Corey realized he might be just a bit too relaxed for her, but let him move in with her, only to spend two years trying to kick him out.

When her now-husband proposed, he took Corey to a minor-league baseball game (they are both baseball fans) and proposed on bended knee during the seventh-inning stretch—with a beautiful ring that he pretended to find in his Cracker Jack box.

With his love, heart, and companionship being the greatest gift he can give you, it *is* the thought that counts. Not every guy is creative, not every guy is romantic, not every guy has the financial resources to "pull out all the stops" when he proposes. But any guy worth marrying should be able to demonstrate through his proposal just how well he knows you and understands and cherishes your unique qualities.

I Can't Believe I Did That! I accepted my first proposal with an "I guess . . ." Pat put on a good show, sure, but he didn't have a ring (note: I did *not* require a diamond, but come on, *any* ring, even a promise ring, would've sufficed). Furthermore, he hadn't asked my father's permission (knowing full well that that was the surest way into his good graces with my Greek family, where he'd never really been "in" to begin with); and he had told our group of friends he was planning on doing it (and they weren't very subtle that they knew something was up). So I had that added pressure. Needless to say, after three years of a stalled engagement with not a single down payment or deposit made on any kind of ceremony, I called it off. He had wasted enough of my time and life. I don't know why he bothered to ask in the first place.—Jenny

Another thing to consider in accepting a lame proposal is how much of the wedding-planning legwork he'll be willing to put in. If his efforts are already half-assed, chances are he's not going to be too into orchestrating The Big Day with you. Not only will this make things frustrating and difficult for you, it is a huge statement as to how unsupportive he is likely to be as your husband. While not every guy has to get into being a wedding planner, he should at least assist you in what needs to be done. If he's not excited about your big day together, then why should you be? Why would you want to put all this effort into somebody who is proving to be nothing more than a schmuck?

Instead of accepting the lame proposal . . .

- Say no.
- Tell him you need time to think about it. Then think about it—hard.
- Don't be afraid to tell him the truth—that you wish you could accept, but that you're disappointed in the way he proposed.
- Go on a relationship hiatus to reconnect with your worthwhile self.

#8 ... Never ask your girlfriend to be part of a threesome.

A pleasure shared is doubled. And who better to share your pleasures than your partner *and* a friend, even in the sack? But even those with the best free love, who truly know how to love the one they're with, may find sharing a partner's pleasuring of a friend or by a friend a bit too much to handle.

Having a threesome, or ménage à trois, can be tricky territory for most ordinary couples to navigate, despite its potential thrills. Even the most solid couples can find their foundations rocked and their love tested with the drama a threesome or moresome can invite. Add a friend to the mix and it can be a too-close-for-comfort recipe for disaster. Even in situations guided by honest, open communication, a threesome can evoke unexpected and complicated feelings of jealousy, inadequacy, and doubt. Any of the partners may find themselves sorting through negative feelings (e.g., I can't believe she did *that*) and assumptions (e.g., he's into her more than me).

In general, threesomes can be exciting. It's a way some adventurous couples fulfill each other's fantasies, or address temptations they might have to cheat. While you might turn to a friend for a threesome because it seems like the comfortable or safe thing to do, in a world full of interesting, sexy people you can enjoy a threesome with, why risk a relationship that's important to you by doing it with a friend? Those lingering, nagging questions and concerns that can easily result from a threesome involving a friend are just not worth it. So instead, visit a swingers club, which is an easier way to find people who are on the same sexual page as you are, or hop on the Internet to find communities that support threesomes and people who are looking for such opportunities with no strings—or drama—attached.

A final note: As in any sexual experience, the risks of an unintended pregnancy and sexually transmitted infection(s) may come into play—in this case, times three!—and these are issues that can really test a romantic relationship, let alone a friendship. When sex play takes on a degree of jeopardy, do you really want to be a potential player in your friend's sexual or emotional health? Or have her put your own at risk?

Never ask your friend to be part of a threesome UNLESS . . .

She has readily indicated that she would be up for some tag-team action.

- *You're* truly attracted to her and want to be intimate with her. This is an even better "unless" if you're planning on ditching your guy in the near future, perhaps for her.
- You're not that close and you don't care that she may not want to be your friend after you ask her.
- Your friend is a he—and your boyfriend has no qualms about a threesome involving more testosterone.

#9 ... Never go after him if he has a girlfriend or wife.

Every now and then you can come across a guy who is absolutely fabulous, and who is—no surprise—taken. Whether married, cohabiting, or in a relationship, it is best not to go after him, no matter how much you find yourself lusting after, fantasizing about, or falling in love with him. Heed such warning even more if he is happy with his partner. Chasing after him or forcing yourself on him is only going to cause distress for you, for him, and for his partner. No good comes out of it. Ever.

If you go after him, you will be a certified home wrecker, and while you may have won the prize (him) temporarily, you won't look like much of a prize when all the dust settles. Even if you don't see it (or hear about it), others will fault you for being selfish and deliberately hurtful. So as tempted as you may be, just leave it alone—say bye-bye. Distance yourself from him as much as possible, especially if you're falling in love with him. If you're meant to be together, let him come after you—and only when he is a free agent. Tell him you're not playing unless you're the only two in his sandbox. Otherwise, go out and find a man of your own. An eligible, unattached one.

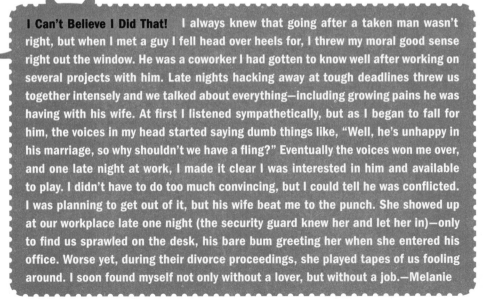

I Can't Believe I Did That!   I always knew that going after a taken man wasn't right, but when I met a guy I fell head over heels for, I threw my moral good sense right out the window. He was a coworker I had gotten to know well after working on several projects with him. Late nights hacking away at tough deadlines threw us together intensely and we talked about everything—including growing pains he was having with his wife. At first I listened sympathetically, but as I began to fall for him, the voices in my head started saying dumb things like, "Well, he's unhappy in his marriage, so why shouldn't we have a fling?" Eventually the voices won me over, and one late night at work, I made it clear I was interested in him and available to play. I didn't have to do too much convincing, but I could tell he was conflicted. I was planning to get out of it, but his wife beat me to the punch. She showed up at our workplace late one night (the security guard knew her and let her in)—only to find us sprawled on the desk, his bare bum greeting her when she entered his office. Worse yet, during their divorce proceedings, she played tapes of us fooling around. I soon found myself not only without a lover, but without a job.—Melanie

#10 ... Never hide your natural smell.

Smell can be an animalistic, instinctual, sexual arouser. Distinct personal scent is actually one of the main influences on our choice of whom we have sex with and how often. Centuries ago, Austrian villagers realized the importance of pheromones and body odor in being a successful attractant. During village dances, they'd often keep handkerchiefs under their armpits, using them later to attract a mate. Even French prostitutes in the 1800s recognized the power of their "parfum de femme," dabbing their own vaginal fluids behind their ears to help woo potential customers with their "wares." Sexy!

Fast-forward to modern times—and the scent of our skin can still be a signature quality, and also quite arousing. Think about it: If somebody smells good, he or she is that much more attractive to you, regardless of what the person looks like, especially for those first few seconds you inhale the intoxicating

> **AND THAT'S A FACT:** On the whole, the partners that smell best to us are those whose genetically based immunity to disease differs most from our own. The sexiest smells humans produce are aromatic by-products of our immune systems!

fragrance. Your sense of smell overrides everything. Not surprisingly, smell triggers our memory, learning, emotions, and moods more than our other senses do; it impacts us the most.

Yet despite such support for your au naturel state, many women try to cover up how they might smell "down there," using feminine sprays, perfume-y soaps, and douches to "freshen up." What they often don't realize is that not only are they making themselves more susceptible to yeast infections, which will definitely put a woman out of her game for a few days, but they're messing with Mother Nature's means to seduce a man. Research indicates that female pheromones in vaginal secretions influence a man's perception of a woman and may induce hormonal changes. So covering up your natural odor not only indicates an insecurity with your body, which is totally *not* sexy, but may impede your full potential in turning him on while dancing, working out, or in the sack!

Look, if you smell funky because you need a bath, have a bath. Or better yet, have a bath with your partner! But if you're just paranoid about how you smell "down there," forget about it. All that those "floral garden," "passion fruit," "sea breeze" smell-hiders will do is alert your partner that *you* think you smell bad. Think of it this way. If you give off a clean, natural smell of exactly who you are, you are inviting potential partners who would by nature be attracted to you to do their best to woo you. We're all just a bunch of animals, after all, sniffing around looking for mates!

#11 ... Never try to get some action when your parents are in the vicinity.

Even if you have no issues with sex, your parents have no qualms about sex, and you're old enough and mature enough to be having sex, trying to get some action when your parents are around is not hot. Families have enough issues in dealing with the fact that everyone's a sexual being, let alone dealing with a good visual reminder of what that really means. While everyone's sexuality should be honored and respected, reminding your parents of yours with moans of pleasure, the banging of your headboard, and just plain too much information about what you're up to is not likely to be well received.

Parents and their children of all ages, in general, do not like getting into the nitty-gritty details of their love lives, much less being made uncomfortably aware that you have one. It not only makes everyone involved feel a little queasy, but it's also inappropriate and shows disrespect to your parents.

But enough about them! No matter how eager you are to get your hands on each other or how much you *think* you like the thrill of possibly getting caught or how much you've fantasized about doing it in your childhood bed, when it comes right down to it, the effect of your parents lurking about within earshot can do a number on your sex drive. For most women, especially if they're not truly comfortable during sex play, the

I Can't Believe I Did That!   When my family went on vacation back in high school, my parents allowed my boyfriend, Tim, to come along. We had one of those big Jeeps, where my parents sat up front, my siblings sat in the first row of seats, and my boyfriend and I sat in the back row. As we drove along, Tim and I lay down in our seat and feigned taking a nap. What we were really doing under that blanket was so wrong given that young peeps and my parents were just inches away! At the time, it seemed like a good, thrilling idea since it was such a bad-ass, sexy, rebellious thing to do. But then, as I tried to stifle my orgasm, my mom asked if we were being good in this knowing tone. I knew I had been found out when she hardly looked at me, let alone hardly said a word to me, for the rest of the trip. It ruined everyone's vacation—and any desire to get with Tim for the rest of the holiday.—Holly sexual response cycle will shut down. With parents close by, a woman can have trouble getting aroused and allowing herself to let go enough to climax. And the same can be true for her guy, with him unable to fully execute or stay hard. While being close to a partner can be satisfying, if you want your motor roaring, there are better times to do it than when your parents are in the next room. Save your sexual shenanigans for when you're back on your own parent- and sibling-free turf. Or, as the old saying goes, "Get a room!"

Instead of trying to get some action when your parents are around . . .

- Take your action to the great outdoors—as long as that doesn't mean *their* backyard.
- Use the time you're spending around your parents to be physically close in nonsexual ways.
- See this momentary abstinence as an opp to get all charged up for when the two of you can finally be alone!

Never try to get some action when your parents are around UNLESS . . .

- They are hard of hearing.
- They *really* are hippy dippy anything-goes about sex.

- You don't care if you get caught. In fact, you thrive off the excitement of possibly getting busted!
- You live with them and it's the only way you can get some with privacy, albeit limited.
- Your culture approves of your mother witnessing the consummation of your marriage.

#12 ... Never lead him on if you're not interested.

Somebody having a crush on you is flattering. The human ego is such that we like fawning attention and we appreciate someone making efforts to please us. Plus, having somebody trying to win you over gives you and your girlfriends plenty to talk about. Even if you're not interested, it's nice to know someone out there thinks you're desirable. Yet though you may love basking in the efforts of your wannabe frog prince, his fawning over you becomes nothing more than unbelievably annoying if you're not really interested.

While it may seem harmless, leading someone on is simply cruel and only invites trouble. Humoring someone's affections, giving false signals that the affections are mutual, and being basically careless with someone's heart will only end up causing pain. Besides hurting him, you could make him angry and unleash a fury of negative repercussions against you, ranging from lingering sore feelings to full-scale retaliation. You never know what someone's capable of when feeling that dangerous combination of hurt and anger, with a dash of humiliation.

If you don't see this one-way attraction going anywhere, let the guy know it—before he thinks it's going somewhere. Start

I Can't Believe I Did That! I had dated this guy, J.P., for a couple of months and it just didn't work out. I was heartbroken and longed for the opportunity to make him realize what he had lost. When his friend, Alan, asked me to go out with him, I thought that it was a great opportunity to make J.P. jealous. Alan was the nicest guy, the perfect gentleman, and a super conversationalist, but I had no attraction to him whatsoever. While on our date, Alan took me to this quaint café, where he ordered an appetizer platter of the yummiest foods, including garlic and olives, which I knew better than to touch on a date—normally. Given the way Alan was looking at me, the subtle touches he was giving me, and his inquiries about whether or not I was a good kisser, I knew I needed a way to botch the date without offending, while I subtly tried to pump him for juice on J.P. Back at Alan's place, seeing that he was looking to get a little closer to me, I started breathing deeper, intentionally stirring up all of the smelly foods in my system. Alan started kissing me, but, as planned, my breath reeked of the garlic, olives, and other nibblies. I thought he was going to hurl when he stopped suddenly and looked at me. I was out the door in no time, realizing I couldn't torture the poor guy anymore.—Gwynn by working the following hints into your conversation: "I love being single right now" or "I'm so focused on my job these days that I can't even think about a relationship" or "I'm just at a point in my life where I want to focus on me." If he simply doesn't want to get a clue, be direct—something along the lines of "I'm really flattered that you're interested, but I'm afraid we're not on the same page with this one." Make no apologies. Don't give reasons that are personal, such as "I don't like your style." This is just how you feel and nothing more needs to be elaborated upon, unless you've shared kisses or more. Then you'll have some explaining to do.

Instead of leading him on . . .

- Set him up with a friend who would make a better match.
- Say out loud that you only want to be friends.
- Make a point of always hanging out in groups. Eventually, he'll get the hint.

Never lead him on UNLESS . . .

- You're not really sure about your feelings for him and need to get to know him better. The issue of attraction is not always perfectly straightforward.
- He led you on first and needs a dose of his own medicine.

#13 ... Never show up on his doorstep after a night of drinking.

Excessive drinking can bring out all our true colors—our vulnerabilities, regrets, anger, passion, love, the whole rainbow of human emotions—in Technicolor! After a few rum and Cokes or gin and tonics, it can be all too easy to let it all out—the good, the bad, and the ugly. If you ever want a night to remember (which will, inevitably, become the night you'll long to forget), all you need is some booze, some of your best male-bashing girlfriends, and a bone to pick with your former Romeo to get yourself into a lot of trouble.

To put it delicately, most women are more of a mess than a class act when they get soused. No matter how empowered or how hot you feel when you've got a buzz going, know that that's only how *you* see you. Depending on how much alcohol you have pumping through your liver, others are seeing you as a drunk or the chick who must've skipped her AA meeting—

and neither are terribly flattering. So if you feel a tough girl act coming on, use the buddy system to make sure nothing regrettable happens, including drunk-dialing past flings or longing for a past love who looks better through beer goggles.

I Can't Believe I Did That! After an unsuccessful long-distance relationship, Nate and I ended up being in the same city for grad school. I was glad for the chance to rekindle, but he ended up stringing me along because he was secretly seeing another ex-girlfriend at the same time. One night I went out for sushi with Zack, Nate's roommate, and we ended up drinking up a storm. I could tell that Zack was digging me, but as we put away more sake, my game plan was to get back to their place and confront Nate about his snakeishness. Once at his front door, I started making out with Zack, thinking it'd be a nice way to get back at Nate as I "accidentally" brushed up against the doorbell. To say that did not go over well with either guy is putting it mildly. As soon as Zack realized I was using him, he darted behind Nate, who slammed the door after calling me some awful profanities. Drunk and hysterical, I kept calling Nate on both the apartment phone and his cell like some lunatic, telling him to come out so that we could talk. He refused. Then he turned off both phones. I was a mess, crying and causing a scene on the stoop, just waiting for the chance that perhaps their other roommate would let me in. The whole incident was so bad on all levels. Drinking and dropping in on an ex are *never* a good mix. —Carly

Also, don't suddenly decide to give your boyfriend an unexpected visit and spring yourself on him in this state—you won't be your best self, and this is a side of you he may not want to get to know! Call a friend when you get ripped and have her talk you out of showing up on his doorstep. Or have your friend escort you home to ensure you take no detours. Hand your friend your cell phone to eliminate the possibility of any drunk calls. Don't let the thought of seeing any former or current guy even cross your mind, unless you're ready to pay the social, emotional, and not-so-romantic consequences. Best advice: drink lots of water and go to bed. As soon as your head hits the pillow, none of it will matter, at least for the moment, anymore.

#14 ... Never throw yourself into his hobbies if they're not your cup of tea.

All too often, people lose themselves in relationships. Their partner's activities, passions, and interests become their activities, passions, and interests. And this is fine if you find yourself truly embracing something your lover is into. What's not okay is if you pretend to be into something you're not, especially in an effort to get him to like you more. Not only are you torturing yourself, but the insincerity will ultimately affect the relationship. Furthermore, the longer you keep up the charade, the harder it will be to untangle yourself from it—that is, excuse yourself from not joining him at the shooting range, ham radio fest, or Shakespeare Museum (where you will miserably fail at Guess Who Said What Shakespeare Quote).

Of course, there are times when he may just want your company as he enjoys his hobby, and you may want to be there with him, simply for support or to bask in the pleasure of his company. But do not apologize if it needs to be more in spirit than actually being there, fully engaged in the activity. Drawing your boundaries—as far as your activities versus his hobbies versus joint ventures goes—can help the two of you to dodge conflict and shows respect in giving each other the time and space needed for doing your own thing. Sometimes being too into each other's activities can make for some relationship

I Can't Believe I Did That!   I asked my date to take me rock climbing since I knew that he was really into it. I thought that maybe if I did it, despite not being terribly interested in it, he would think that I was cool and worth getting more involved with. What I didn't mention to him, however, is that I'm afraid of heights. Thinking that we would start out with something "easy," I felt the fear of God in me as I looked up-up-up the beautiful, steep rocky mountainside of Seneca Rocks, West Virginia. Not wanting to chicken out after having come all this way, I put on my gear, tried to pay attention through the instructions, which were a matter of life or death, and started to climb. And I was doing okay—until I looked down. I started sweating and practically crapped the way an animal does when it is scared to death. I just started tooting away in fear, my butt just inches from my date's face! And I was completely paralyzed from going any farther. Needless to say, we didn't try that—or anything else—again.—Shauna claustrophobia. Every couple needs time apart to help keep the passion alive for when they're together! Relationships can quickly go down hill when the two lovers are codependent and inseparable. Plus, a relationship cannot and will not be sustainable if it's built on false impressions. People can only take so much, and there will be a day when he will realize that you've had it with getting dragged to Star Trek conventions—like when you finally crack, hurling his starship figurine collection at him when he suggests naming your firstborn "Spock." So pick activities to do together that you both truly enjoy. Leave the rest to each other to enjoy alone or with other like-minded aficionados.

Never throw yourself into his hobbies UNLESS . . .

- Trying an activity or two of his—even just once—will make him happy.
- You don't know whether or not you will like it.
- It promises great quality time—and will serve as a "gentle" reminder to him that you are his favorite thing to "do."
- Your humoring him guarantees rewards under the sheets that eve!

#15 ... Never use the toilet in front of your partner.

Some couples feel that they should be able to do and say anything in front of each other, even if it's not always so pretty. And it's true, with closeness in a relationship comes an ease and openness about certain things that early in a relationship you'd never dream of doing in front of your partner—using your menstrual heating pad, flossing, adjusting your thong along your butt crack, or picking at a pimple, for instance. However, most people would agree that there needs to be some sort of limit in what a lover, in particular, is exposed to. This is especially true when it comes to using the loo. There are just some things you don't need to know about each other—or at least share—and the vision of doing a #2 tops the list.

Even if you're comfortable with your bodily functions, are comfortable with each other, and are comfortable bearing all, carefully consider all the ways in which using the bathroom in front of each other can provide too much information. Fully exposing that you're human in your need to pee and poop can cause you to plummet from goddess to mere mortal status.

And let's just lay it out here. Even if people are okay with peeing in front of each other, the chances of being, er, flatulent are quite good, especially for him (you know what I'm talking about—some men become the Pied Piper once they close the bathroom door). Mood killer! Mystery and aura destroyer!

In sum, some things are better kept to yourself. That includes using the toilet, changing your tampon (guaranteed to make him hurl), and any and all other ablutions that fall

I Can't Believe I Did That! My partner and I were on a weeklong glacier camping trek. It was really hard to use the bathroom when one needed to go, so we both held out doing #2 until we could bear the pains of impending bowel movements no more. As a snowstorm raged around our tent, we grabbed a plastic bag and took turns pooping into it. He was a gentleman in letting me go first, but it was definitely not the most romantic moment in the world. While a very humbling experience that we occasionally laugh about (but would rather forget), I never want to be that up-close and personal again!—Jill under the category of personal hygiene (they call it personal for a reason!). Unless hanging out in the john watching you poop is his fetish (and that's a whole different story/different book!), save your together time in the bathroom for hot shower sex.

#16 ... Never lie about cheating.

There was a news story about a female detective in Atlanta who busts cheaters. Her clients, mostly women, hire her to spy on their boyfriends or spouses to confirm that these guys are cheating. In almost all cases, the clients knew and just needed the proof—whether or not they'd confronted their lover about their suspicions. In all of the cases, the detective's clients were never wrong. The lesson in this: if you're cheating, chances are your partner knows. And if you think your partner doesn't know, chances are, sooner or later, you will get busted. Private investigators aside, when people cheat, they get careless, and when they get careless, they leave clues, and clues get you caught.

More than the threat of getting caught is the plain wrongness of cheating, and the lying you have to do to pull it off. Whether or not you still love your partner or have fallen out of love, it's the dishonesty that is the poison you're willingly introducing to your relationship. The cheating hurts, but the lying is what does the real and lasting damage to trust, which is the most important part of your relationship—more important than love itself to many people. Even if you think you have good reasons to lie about being unfaithful—you love your partner, you don't want to separate, you have a child together, you need the security he provides, you want to keep up appearances (not letting word out that you're a cheater)—lying about a wrong never makes it all right. It never makes any of it right.

So if you've been getting your game somewhere else, come clean. It will show that you have more respect for the relationship and partner than your actions let on, especially if you

I Can't Believe I Did That! I was involved with a doctor, but cheating on him. He had suspected and asked me, but I lied about it since I really didn't know how I felt about him and our future together. I ended up getting totally busted when he thanked me for giving him a nasty little STD that he'd never had before he met me. I just died because I had no clue that the man I'd been messing around with on the side had infected me! I don't know which was worse at the time—finding out I had an infection or being caught in a lie. Now, in retrospect, I don't know if the bigger lesson learned was never lie about cheating, or never lie about cheating when you're dating a doctor!—Deb hope the relationship to continue in spite of your indiscretion. If you're confronted with your partner's suspicions and you've just been busted, don't add insult to injury by continuing to lie about it. It's the first step in dealing with the issues in your relationship that led to your affair, whether that ultimately makes or breaks the relationship.

Never lie about cheating UNLESS . . .

- You're breaking up with the person. Do they really need to know in the long run? It may just end up causing a lot more unnecessary pain.
- You already are the bad guy in being the dumper.
- Your relationship wasn't clearly defined as monogamous, so it could technically not be deemed cheating. Why wake the sleeping giant if he can lie there?
- You're ready to deal with karma—and it can be a bitch!

#17 ... Never show jealousy.

Whether you're just a little smitten or head over heels in love, it can be hard not to show jealousy when somebody is flirting with your guy or spending a lot of time with him. It can be equally hard when he's innocently showing interest in others or is still grappling with past love affairs, even if former lovers are no longer a threat. After all, we're culturally conditioned to protect our heart's "territory," and jealousy is among the first defenses to spring into action when we feel threatened. Unfortunately, it's also the least effective defense and one of the hardest emotions to keep in check. Jealousy seems like a natural way to express how much you care about someone. But it's really an expression of fear, insecurity, envy, inadequacy, and a whole host of other qualities that are not very attractive or healthy or good for your relationship.

People are more likely to experience jealousy if they don't feel good about themselves—or their relationship. If you're jealous by nature, don't beat yourself up; rather, try to understand its destructiveness and work hard on not letting your emotions get the best of you. Jealousy is *your* problem, not his, no matter how much you blame his behavior for it. It's yours

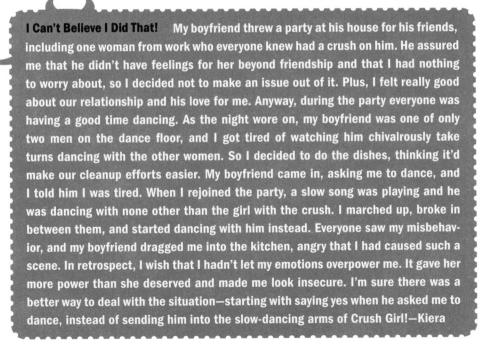

I Can't Believe I Did That! My boyfriend threw a party at his house for his friends, including one woman from work who everyone knew had a crush on him. He assured me that he didn't have feelings for her beyond friendship and that I had nothing to worry about, so I decided not to make an issue out of it. Plus, I felt really good about our relationship and his love for me. Anyway, during the party everyone was having a good time dancing. As the night wore on, my boyfriend was one of only two men on the dance floor, and I got tired of watching him chivalrously take turns dancing with the other women. So I decided to do the dishes, thinking it'd make our cleanup efforts easier. My boyfriend came in, asking me to dance, and I told him I was tired. When I rejoined the party, a slow song was playing and he was dancing with none other than the girl with the crush. I marched up, broke in between them, and started dancing with him instead. Everyone saw my misbehavior, and my boyfriend dragged me into the kitchen, angry that I had caused such a scene. In retrospect, I wish that I hadn't let my emotions overpower me. It gave her more power than she deserved and made me look insecure. I'm sure there was a better way to deal with the situation—starting with saying yes when he asked me to dance, instead of sending him into the slow-dancing arms of Crush Girl!—Kiera to indulge—at your peril—or to refuse to let own you, though it may take a lot of practice to tame this beast. If you trust the feelings you and your partner have for each other, jealousy will not be able to find a foothold. Learn how to communicate effectively in talking about issues that might provoke jealousy. Let him know when somebody else's behaviors, or his reactions to them, are bothering you. He cannot fault you for the way you feel, but the way you handle things is very much in your control, which means keeping cool even if you're seething with jealousy inside. Be conscious of it when it does arise, and learn to talk yourself down from it. Stay away from situations that may invite jealousy, because it only damages relationships. If he's somebody who wants to make you jealous in order to feel more secure about the relationship or your love for him, or if he gets off on just plain being cruel, get rid of him. No guy's need for an ego or an ego trip is worth putting yourself through the torture of regularly wrestling with jealousy.

#18 ... Never get below-the-belt piercings.

Unless you like intense pain and want to risk decreased sensation and the possibility of acquiring an infection, piercing any of the jewels in your box is not for you. With most women's sexual anatomies not suited for a clitoral piercing—specifically, not strong enough to support the weight of the jewelry—women seeking this type of adornment will often go for having another nether area pierced in such a way that the jewelry presses up against their love knob for greater sensation during sex. While piercing the 8,000 nerves that make up the clitoris may make for more sensation during sex for those willing to go there, the pain of having this area pierced is a bit too much for most, and doesn't always turn out well. In having this area overstimulated with the piercing, some women actually report less sensation as they adapt to the state of their wares. Regardless of what gets pierced down there, a woman risks a nasty infection, which can become serious if left untreated.

I Can't Believe I Did That! I have had a couple of piercings—one on my tongue and one in my navel—and have never had problems with them as far as keeping them clean and infection-free. Since my tongue stud was such a turn-on during oral sex with my boyfriend, we thought it'd be really cool for me to get my clitoris pierced. It hurt unbelievably, but I still thought it'd be worth it—until it got infected. I have never been in so much pain down there—or as unsightly. I used to take pride in my "attributes," but suddenly I was looking at something so gross, all pus-like, crusty, and irritated. Of course, my boyfriend wanted nothing to do with me down there, not that I could've withstood him touching me anyway. So something that was supposed to improve our sex lives ended up benching us for a while. I ended up just taking it out and letting the hole heal.—Ana

Considering that your chances of suffering serious pain, desensitization, and infection with a clitoral piercing are fairly high, how about you skip it and find other ways to juice up your sex life? If you're dead set on getting a piercing, consider the highly erogenous nipples instead, as they're not as likely to keep you celibate for a couple of weeks (though this kind of piercing can make you want to go topless for a while, with thrill seekers reporting razorblade sensations when fabric rubs against the piercing). Other options include wearing Venus

Butterfly or remote-controlled thongs that provide vibrator action against your clit at any time, without the risks a hole invites. There are tons of ways to pleasure your clitoris without sporting jewelry—just take the time to experiment! It can take a lifetime to explore all the wonderful potential for pleasure, and you don't need any piercing to do it. So what are you waiting for?

Instead of getting a below-the-belt piercing . . .

- Get something else pierced.
- Consider a tattoo.
- Love your vulva and all of its erotic potential for what it is. Your downtown Disneyland doesn't need enhancements!

> **AND THAT'S A FACT:** In a study of male and female intimate body piercings (including nipple and genital piercings), an overwhelming majority of participants said that the reasons for obtaining piercings included uniqueness, self-expression, and sexual expression. While more than 75 percent of participants reported that they still liked their piercings, more than half of all participants also reported health concerns including site sensitivity, skin irritation, and a change or discomfort in urinary flow.

#19 ... Never abstain from sex just because you're having your period.

For some women, the week of their period is their horniest time of the month. If you're one of them, part of this regular sexual peak could be that you feel more sexually liberated during this time, since the possibility of pregnancy is somewhat diminished. Or you may be experiencing a little pelvic congestion, which may make you feel more aroused. Or you may be feeling more feline, feminine, and sexual because your menstrual flow symbolizes fertility in an "I am woman, hear me roar" kind of way. Or maybe you've found that orgasm relieves menstrual symptoms, like cramps, so you're all over him for a little natural pain relief (hey, he doesn't need to know he's better than your over-the-counter options).

Robyn is a big proponent of sex during her period: "I love that my boyfriend doesn't have a problem with it. We both think that the fact that neither of us takes issue is totally sexy.

We bond over being able to do something that some people can't handle—something that should be perfectly natural given it's simply a part of being a woman. I've had some of the best sex and relieved some of my worst menstrual woes in going for it during my time of the month."

Given all of the plusses for period sex, don't let issues that you or your partner have concerning "that time of the month" keep you from having some of the best sex of your life. Can having sex while you're having your period be messy? Sure. But is it dirty? No! It's nature doing what it does, and it's just one more rhythm and flow you should just go with. No need to hole up like a nun for a week. Make it clear to your partner you're game if he is—it may become a special time of month for both of you. Just make sure that you have lubricant handy (despite providing natural "lube," a woman's menstrual flow actually causes a slight drying effect), and make shower play a part of postsex bonding.

If either one of you is uncomfortable having intercourse when you've got the dot, don't punish yourself by abstaining altogether. You can take your action into the bath or shower, which keeps things neat. Or relive your high school days and dry hump each other!

Never abstain from sex during your period UNLESS . . .

- It goes against your religious beliefs.
- It's causing you more discomfort than pleasure.
- You're on top of sheets that you'd rather not risk staining.
- You don't have a condom and/or other form of birth control handy. (A woman's cervix opens up more for the passage of blood, actually increasing the chance of getting knocked up or acquiring sexually transmitted infections, including HIV.)

#20 ... Never apologize . . .

- For your feelings.
- For your wants and needs.
- For your beliefs.
- For being a woman.
- For doing things the old-fashioned way.
- For going against the grain.
- For standing up for your rights.
- For doing what makes you—and not everyone else—happy.
- For your PMS.
- For your sexual orientation.
- For what you will and won't do in bed.
- For wanting more out of a partner and a relationship.
- For needing to put your school or career ahead of a relationship.
- For not wanting kids.

- For wanting kids.
- For needing a break from your kids—or someone else's.
- For not being in the mood.
- For wanting to stay home and chill instead of go out.
- For your past.
- For your sex drive.
- For your friends.
- For *his* mistakes.
- For needing to break up with him.
- For deciding to stay with him when he has wronged you.
- For your issues.
- For being who you are.
- For needing to find out who you are.

Never apologize UNLESS . . .

- You're truly in the wrong.
- You said something hurtful in anger, even if it's true.
- Kissing it will make it better. One partner always needs to be the "bigger" person.

#21 ... Never write your ex a letter letting him know "how you feel."

You're driving along and hear "your" song on the radio, and even though you haven't been a couple for some time, and you thought you'd let go of him ages ago, the memories begin to tug at your heartstrings. And then, after a few days of seeing his name everywhere, or his "twins" in the most unexpected places, you begin to wonder if some universal force is nudging you to contact him. Maybe he's been thinking about you. Maybe *he's* being bombarded with reminders of *you*. Maybe he's just been waiting for *you* to make the move—to say what is obviously on both your minds, that you were meant to be together/that breaking up was all a mistake/that all is forgiven. Maybe the universe is starting to stir, telling you that he is indeed The One.

Yes, these are all the thoughts that run through your head, the "signs" you read or misread, and the shreds of fleeting hope that can lead you to write one of those infamous "ex" letters. Put down that pen. Step away from that keyboard. This is definitely one of those "somebody stop me" moments that you ignore at your own peril.

If you are meant to be together, you will make your way back to each other much the same way you found each other in the first place, not as the result of some weepy, desperate soul-bearing in the form of a letter. There is a reason they call them breakups, you know. You're breaking off and moving on—with an emphasis on the moving on part. Writing your ex a letter will get in the way of your moving on. In fact, if you cave at this point, after all of the work you've done in getting yourself to a better place, you'll probably reverse all the healing and progress you've made since breaking up. You'll relive all the pain, make yourself vulnerable to more pain by putting your heart out there unprotected, and you'll probably get caught in a roller-coaster ride of unrealistically high hopes and anguished disappointment. And all of it unnecessary because you shouldn't have written that dumb "I miss you, I still love you, I can't live without you" letter in the first place. So don't do it. He's put you through enough. If it's meant to happen again, let him make the first move.

Instead of writing your ex a letter . . .

- Handwrite (don't type because it will be too tempting to e-mail) a letter, but write it only for yourself, and burn it.
- Call your friends and have them remind you of all the reasons you broke up in the first place.
- Record what you want to say, then play it back to yourself. You won't like what you hear, even if you have the best of intentions or highest hopes for reconciliation.

#22 ... Never continue dating him if he openly lusts after other women.

Your father has always had a thing for Candice Bergen. Occasionally, when she pops up on the television screen, he teases your mother about his thing for the actress, to which your mom chuckles and responds, "She's a beautiful woman" or "Yeah, sure, dear, good luck getting that one." Between their mutual appreciation of her beauty, the fact that he would likely never meet her, and mom feeling secure in her relationship with her husband, his thing for Candice is nothing more than a joke. It is certainly not a threat to their relationship.

It's one thing for your guy to notice an obviously attractive woman, or even to be a "fan" à la Dad and Candice Bergen. It's another for him to be slobbering and drooling and going on and on about how hot she is, as if you're not even there, being made to feel like a plate of chopped liver. Some men are thoughtless in their commentary or even intentionally cruel in letting their partner know that they find another woman attractive. Some men think that, despite the fact that the comments are hurtful, openly lusting after other women is socially supported macho behavior that his partner shouldn't take issue with if he isn't actually actively pursuing the object of his desire. Some men simply don't care that they are so tell-all in their lustful longing—they know that they sit in the driver's seat where the relationship is concerned, and this kind of disrespect is something she's willing to put up with since she's lucky to be with him.

This isn't a case of your guy having a little "thing" for Eva Longoria, or the occasional appreciative glance at a striking woman. This is chronic, thoughtless, hurtful, and inappropriate harping on his sophomoric fantasies—at the expense of your feelings. The constant ogling of other women translates as a putdown, and is absolutely unacceptable, especially when in the presence of a lady. Think of this bad habit of his as like any other bad habit that you find intolerable and that's not going away. Because all relationships are optional, just say "no, thanks" to this one. It's that simple.

Unfortunately, when a woman doesn't feel good about herself, when she's afraid of losing her partner, or when she'd rather be involved than on her own, she will put up with it, no matter how degrading or how much damage it does to her ego. Cynthia can attest to this: "I met this guy online and I guess he figured that since that's the way we met that I was desperate and couldn't get anyone else. Within a couple of weeks of meeting, he was already checking out other women in front of me, making me feel like crap. I told him it bothered me, but he acted like he didn't hear me. It was really important to me to have a boyfriend at the time, so I tolerated it for a while until one of my friends took issue with it when he did it in front of her. At that point I realized just how disrespectful and bad it was—and that I had to get rid of him."

If you're in this kind of relationship, the kind where you're being disrespected by your lover gawking other women or otherwise letting you know how hot he thinks they are, put your foot down or get out! If he's not willing to show you the respect you deserve, do what Cynthia did, and show him the door.

Instead of dating a guy who lusts after other women . . .

- Have a no-tolerance policy. Dump him.
- Give him one chance to start acting right. Tell him to keep his thoughts to himself or you're out.
- Lust after other men in front of him to give him a taste of his own medicine.

#23 ... Never freak at the sight of an uncircumcised penis.

Women tend to be in shock when they see their first penis with a foreskin, that is, one that is not circumcised. Given that most men in the world are *not* snipped, it's rather ironic that a circumcised penis (one where the foreskin has been removed) is regarded as the "norm" simply because it has been the standard in the United States for decades. It's a shame that the circumcised penis has taken center stage in male sexual anatomy presentation, because now a preponderance of Americans think that a circumcised penis is more attractive simply because that is what they're accustomed to seeing. Men who sport the look Mother Nature intended are regularly made to feel like a freak show when they drop their drawers, and women just plain miss out on how much fun it can be to fraternize with an uncircumcised penis.

Should you discover that your new lover has an intact penis, do not ruin your romantic evening by reacting with shock or unease. Remain calm and make friends. This penis, like any other, wants to please you. And if you give it a chance, it's likely to do just that—and in ways you've probably never known. Women have repeatedly noted that they've actually been more sexually satisfied by men with a foreskin, because the foreskin rubs against their G-spot during thrusting, providing much more amazing stimulation than a circumcised penis.

Variety is indeed the spice of life, and if you're lucky enough to find yourself in the company of the uncircumcised variety of penis, then relish the experience. It's the worldwide "secret" to some seriously good sex. Plus, one ingredient of amazing sex

AND THAT'S A FACT: Circumcision rates have steadily been decreasing in the United States, as more parents determine it to be unnecessary, especially when considering the medical costs of childbirth. While there's mixed data on whether or not a foreskin puts a man at increased risk for contracting HIV during unprotected sex (with the most recent long-term study indicating that it does), the overall consensus is that, as long as the foreskin area is kept clean, an uncircumcised penis poses no health risk to the owner or his partner.

is to accept everything about your lover. How would you like it if he thought that your butt was too flat or that your boobs were too droopy or that your labia weren't perfectly symmetrical? And that he couldn't get it on with you because of it? Ridiculous.

Never freak at the sight of an uncircumcised penis UNLESS . . .

You're Jewish, he told you he was Jewish, you want him to be Jewish, and his peepee is proving he's not Jewish.

#24 ... Never fake orgasm.

This one's worth repeating: Never fake orgasm—even if you think faking it is a selfless, compassionate act that will spare his feelings. It absolutely does neither of you any good. All you do is deprive yourself of sexual fulfillment (if climaxing is your goal) and give him a false sense of rock-star status. In basically lying to him about having an orgasm, you end up betraying both your sexual needs and his trust in your sex communication. Just think of how his ego will be blown if he ever finds out—and you thought you were doing it to make him feel good! Believe it or not, most men do not want to be lied to in this arena. It's one of the ultimate sex insults.

In addition, every time you feign climax, you train your body to believe that the fake orgasm is all it's getting. In other words, you develop a habit that desensitizes you and makes it more difficult for you to attain orgasm for real. You end up settling in the sack. That's not the point of sex!

So take the porn-star pressure off of yourself and admit that something isn't working for you, whether it's the position, lack of foreplay, or issues in the relationship. Not having an orgasm should not be interpreted as though somebody is doing something wrong—you just need to play with the recipe a bit more. Sweeten things up, add more spice, let things simmer a little longer. So many factors contribute to success in climaxing, such as stress, relationship comfort, and alcohol consumption, that the onus shouldn't be on one partner entirely. This needs to be a team effort.

I Can't Believe I Did That! Until I had a real orgasm, I used to put on a really exaggerated Meg Ryan-type show—really theatrical with lots of screaming and "Oh God's!" Lots of thrashing and clawing—basically, my impression of losing control during orgasm was being out of control. The last time I did it, I was having sex with this guy on a hotel bed with a headboard. Seeing this as an opportunity for an Oscar-worthy performance, I banged the back of my head against the wooden headboard to the rhythm of our thrusting—and hard. Too hard! I knocked myself out, only to wake up in the hospital. I had the biggest bump on the back of my head, and hurt for days. And no orgasm of my own to show for my pain and trouble. Perhaps the biggest headache was trying to explain to my parents how I ended up in the ER!—Morgan

If you're having trouble attaining orgasm in general, take the time to masturbate. It is the only way to know what turns you on in a way that you can show him. If you're having trouble climaxing when you're with him, see this as an opportunity to discuss what you're doing and how you're doing it (maybe he's more talented with his tongue or maybe you need to try being on top); any sexual and relationship needs that are not being met (you like it rough and he's too gentle); and new things you'd like to try that turn you on (perhaps you're likelier to let go in the great outdoors). See this as an opportunity to bond in sharing and experimenting, while taking the pressure off of your having an orgasm. It will come once you let it, but it won't if you just keep pretending.

Instead of faking orgasm . . .

- Show him how it's done. Get yourself off as you're fooling around.
- Guide his hand over your special spot(s), applying the pressure and rhythm you enjoy so that he can imitate later.
- Don't rush through sex. Take your time getting aroused, relishing your body's reactions and those of your partner.
- Have your vibrator handy as backup. (But see Never #34 first.)

#25 ... Never get married to please someone else.

Currently, the U.S. government provides more than 1,000 benefits to legally married couples. Tax breaks, legal resident status, visiting a partner in prison, and automatic inheritance might be fine perceived incentives to tie the knot. More compelling reasons come in the form of your mother, your grandmother, your coupled friends, your coworkers, and your president and commander in chief—all of whom are pressing, pressing, pressing for you to get hitched. Somewhere in that list of reasons you might get married is love, of course, but you can see why that can sometimes get buried under the weight of all those other reasons—or not be there at all, for the greater importance of those other reasons to some people.

Society definitely rewards people for getting married. The wedding industry, Hollywood love stories, romance novels, and even Las Vegas, have all glamorized "'til death do you part." For many women, their wedding day is supposed to be the best day of their lives—the day they prove to the world that they are worthy of being part of an official pair, Mr. and Mrs., a single-no-more. But the fact is that after all the corks have been popped and the rice has been nibbled up by the birds, you're in for trouble if you haven't gotten married because you want to, for all of your own right reasons. People who get married not for themselves, not for their own happiness, not necessarily because they want to, but because they want to make someone else happy, end up with a prescription for pain.

Just ask Claire's best friend, Julie: "Claire's mother has always put pressure on her to get married and have kids. Her coworkers, mostly married schoolteachers, were just as bad with the 'Why aren't you married?' hectoring. When one of her younger brothers got married and then had a child, the 'Old Maid or marry' pressure from her mother only got worse. Desperate to please her mother, Claire got engaged to the first man she fell into a relationship with. But she had barely told her friends anything about him. That's probably because she has paid for most of his bills since he moved out of his parents' house to move in with her. She doesn't talk about being in love with him the way most women do when they've found the love of their life. Instead, she is always complaining about planning her wedding, the money he owes her, and trying to keep both families happy. We're all certain that she is doing this just to be married and off her mother's badgering radar. It's just so sad because you must know it's not going to end well."

Months or years down the road, stuck in a miserable marriage that happened to please someone else, nobody is happy. Next, these couples are part of the 50 percent of Americans looking to get a divorce. Don't let this happen to you!

Instead of getting married to please someone else . . .

- Chase down your own dreams.
- Make a list of the reasons why you would want to marry anyone (love, friendship, attraction, and so on). If your intended doesn't measure up, don't take the plunge.
- Do everything you would do with or without a partner, just without being officially married.

#26 ... Never ask if it's in yet.

Want to hit him where it hurts? Even if it's not a lot to aim for? Nothing will sock it to him quite like asking him if it's in, especially when it already is! This comes off as the ultimate insult to a man regarding the size of his penis and it really doesn't matter whether it's small, large, or somewhere in between. And even if you have no issues with penis size, asking if it's in would suggest to him that he doesn't know what he's doing or where it's supposed to go. Or if it *is* in, what to do with it! Nothing brings the curtain down on your prospects for a good time faster than this sort of emasculating question. He'll be hurt, humiliated, and, no doubt, no longer in the mood.

As regrettable as hurting his feelings is, the fact is you're responsible for leaving yourself hanging. After some foreplay, working up a sweat, and a pressing desire to pull him into you, this comment can bring things to a screeching halt, with both of you footing the bill of the price paid. With a loin longing to feel him, any sexual frustration you were experiencing before you said this dumb thing is going to be heightened because there will be no magic left in his wand.

Though the attitude may not be politically correct, penis size is important to some women, just like breast size is to some men. If your guy's pride and joy doesn't meet your great expectations, but you still want to be intimate with him, avoid situations and positions where this question pops into your mind.

I Can't Believe I Did That! This situation had "regrettable" written all over it. The guy I was about to have sex with for the first (and last) time takes out an extra-large condom, which was like a billboard drawing attention to his extra-small penis. Then he made some sheepish remark about the friend who fixed him up with the condom who thought quite a lot of his equipment—which only drew more of my attention to his thumb-sized erection. I didn't have high hopes at this point, but soon he was on top of me and having at it . . . I think. I kept waiting and waiting to feel something—anything!—for all the thrusting and panting that was happening on top of me, until, exasperated, I blurted out, "Is it in yet?" which he answered with a grunt, then a sigh as he rolled off of me. Apparently, not only had it been in, he was done already and I never even knew it!—Theresa

Or take control of the situation by guiding his penis with your hand, which is especially easy to do if you're on top. You can also sneak a peek between your legs and try to figure out his coordinates. In other words, stick with situations where you both know it's "in" and you're happy with what comes next!

#27 ... Never be afraid to show him what feels good.

If there's one complaint men voice when it comes to sex, it's that she just lies there. Usually, this desire for something more is described as him wanting a woman who can be a whore in the bedroom. Despite the negative connotation, this isn't a bad thing. What men are really getting at is that they want women to get into it and show them what feels good. A person who is sexually confident, who can show her partner how to touch and where to touch, is absolutely irresistible. Who doesn't want the partner who takes charge and who can drive you crazy with a look or touch that says "I know what I'm doing here"?

The more you and your partner know each other, the better the sex is going to be. This is partly because you're going to know more about what each of you fancies and finds sexually stimulating. If you don't take the time to show one another what feels good, you could be missing out on tons of fun, hot action, and sensual sensations you've never known before. And why deprive yourself of that? Don't let fear hold you back from true pleasure.

While sex seems fairly self-explanatory, everyone is different and has different particulars about what really turns them on or feels good. So speak up! When you reach a moment during sex where you know a slight adjustment would up your pleasure quotient, say so. Or show him by guiding his hand or body to where it would feel good. Say it or do it in a way that lets him know you *are* into it, that you want to feel as good as he does, and he's the man who can make it happen for you.

At the same time, make a point of ascertaining what would make your partner feel good. Questions as simple as "Like this?" or "Does this feel good?" give him the chance to say where he likes to be touched—and how—and shows him you're not just "laying there," that you care about the quality of the experience for both of you. He may also take your lead and ask you what *you* like.

If your partner isn't very open about what turns him into a delirious sexpot, this may take some of your own investigative work. Kaylie found out the fun way when her boyfriend and she were having a sexfest week. As her boyfriend was doing

Kaylie missionary, she spanked him firmly a couple of times. He kind of hesitated, as if surprised, and then Kaylie asked him if what she'd done was okay. He shyly said that he had liked it and later told Kaylie that he'd felt pleasurable sensations throughout his butt and genitals. After that, spanking became a regular part of their lovemaking. What a nice discovery!

So keep your eyes and ears open to anything your partner takes pleasure in. Don't be afraid to use books or "visual aids" to make suggestions or show him what could potentially feel good. You may just bring your sex potential to the next level!

#28 ... Never believe him when he says, "Don't worry, I'll pull out."

How many women have heard this one before? If he doesn't like condoms or doesn't have a condom, but is going to die of blue balls, chances are, you've heard this I-wanna-get-wit-choo line. More officially known as the withdrawal method, pulling out before his Mount St. Helens erupts is the oldest form of birth control around. Yet despite having had a long time to practice, the male species is far from having perfected pulling out, especially when you add alcohol, drugs, fatigue, or pure sexual excitement to the mix. It's a battle with Mother Nature that he's not meant to win. Even if a guy has the most amazing ejaculatory control and can pull out seemingly without spilling a drop, a woman can still get pregnant. This is because there are active sperm in pre-ejaculatory fluid. Many guys who say "Don't worry, I'll pull out" either don't know this or, in the heat of the moment, don't care. They'll take their chances, especially if they think they're more suave and all-powerful in this department than other men.

Accidents happen. The withdrawal method is only 77 percent effective as a form of birth control, and puts you at risk for a whole slew of sexually transmitted diseases, so don't let him talk you into it. Tell him "no condom, no action," no apologies. It's playing on your terms or not playing at all. Because even if he does pull out, as promised, your chances of ending up holding a blue-positive pregnancy test strip in your hand a month later are dangerously good. Don't risk it.

#29 ... Never go overboard on imitating a stripper.

In the age of three-inch platform heels you can buy at the mall, titty tassels you can order online, and pole-dancing classes you can take at the gym, it's hard not to get caught up in imitating the curvy, leggy, "skintillating" moves of many a rocker, rapper, or businessman's favorite—the stripper. Yet in wildly tossing your mane, prowling around like a tigress in heat, and performing splits that put world-class gymnasts to shame, consider well whether certain "ladylike" stage antics are really meant for your bedroom.

Professional performances at the KitKat Club certainly can elicit jaw-dropping reactions. That's partly because strippers are performers. They're paid to put on a show. So they're going to perform circus level, do-not-try-this-at-home feats, and they're going to exaggerate their moves, sounds, and desire to please their audience, especially if they want to make more money. And they do all this knowing that when they're done, they're going to go backstage, change their clothes, and go home to watch Conan O'Brien before going to bed. Which is to say they dance and prance and strip and shimmy in front of a guy, but don't have to deliver on the promise of all those theatrics. You, on the other hand, do. While it can be hot and erotic to seduce your man in stripper fashion, don't put unrealistic expectations upon yourself, or your partner.

If playing stripper is something you know you'd both enjoy, by all means strip away. Just know that the more of a big sexy show you make of it, the more sex-pectations will arise from it. Which might be great—or might be hard to satisfy. Only you know how much game you've both really got.

AND THAT'S A FACT: Health-care professionals in neighborhoods near strip clubs regularly report on the extreme hazards of the strip profession. One Philadelphia dancer's grand finale often sent her to the emergency room to remove shards of broken shot glass "down there," the result of a gyrating split move gone wrong. In Copenhagen, bar strippers "pour" the customers' drinks, legs spread, by way of an alcohol-loaded squirt gun mechanism and gravity's law that what goes up must come down. Talk about a yeast infection waiting to happen.

Furthermore, trying to be a stripper empowers the whole pro-stripper movement we have going on in this country right now. You're basically setting yourself up to be measured against societal and professional standards of what it supposedly means to be a sexy, sexual woman. Don't feel like you need to play into that game, unless, of course, it turns you on and you think you've got a little something to show off.

Instead of imitating a stripper . . .

- Make up your own moves and routine. Show him how it's really done!
- Hire one for a private party.

- Highlight whatever is super sexy about you, whether it's your cooking, painting, or to-die-for massage, and make that your performance.
- Tell him to go out with the guys to get any stripper fever out of his system, as long as he comes home to you. (But see Never #22.)
- Have him strip for *you*.

#30 ... Never have sex on a first date.

Dating rules are generally made to be broken. If a love connection is meant to be, then a couple makes up their own rules—they do what works for them from day—or night—one. Yet there is one rule when it comes to dating that lovelorn hopefuls should heed the first time they go out with somebody: Never have sex on your first date. That's because having sex on a first date puts the whammy on the prospective relationship from the outset. It immediately introduces complicated or unpleasant issues such as miscommunication over postsex expectations; the concerns that you must be a "slut" if you do this with everybody; the that-was-too-easy/game-over factor; or the too-much-too-soon pressure. Shagging too soon can unnecessarily handicap your relationship or even cause it never to become a relationship at all.

This isn't to say, however, that you can't get a little bit of loving. Go ahead and give him a taste, perhaps literally, of what's to be had if and when you get to know each other better. Touch him in ways that will make him want to come back for more. Rest easy knowing that sex is not on the agenda, and this is the time for shameless, infectious, you've-piqued-my-interest flirting. Soak up the good-natured, easygoing fun that can be had without trying to get into each other's pants. You'll never have this time in your relationship again, and if it's meant to last, you'll have plenty of time to deal with the passion and drama that comes with sleeping together. And if he wants more, and tries to get more, then he's not much of a gentleman, which is better discovered sooner than later anyway.

I Can't Believe I Did That! This hot guy I'd been working with asked me out and I felt a little ambivalent about it because my roommate had a crush on him. But he was so hot and I needed the ego boost, so I went out with him. Well, we ended up going back to my place, and one thing led to another. Not only did I end up sleeping with the guy, but we did it on my roommate's bed. I felt like a terrible friend, though karma came swiftly. He and I wound up in this emotionally abusive, cyclical sex-based relationship where he loved and hated me for being a Madonna-whore, in his eyes, all because I'd slept with him on the first date. I was so much of what he desired, but things started off with him the "wrong" way and he faulted me more than himself for that.—Katrine

You have one chance to affect whether a first date becomes a one-night stand or the beginning of a relationship, and *not* having sex on that occasion is the key. Let the relationship become a relationship *before* you introduce sex to the equation. Make out. Hold hands. Have great conversations. And remember, you don't have to wait forever—just as long as it takes for you both to know each other well enough that those complicated misperceptions won't arise.

Never have sex on a first date UNLESS . . .

- You've already known each other for a long time and the date is a formality in establishing your feelings and taking a step forward as more than friends.
- You're both horny and in the mood, but don't see a second date happening—and both of you are cool with that.
- You're at a swinger or other laissez-faire sex event where such rules of engagement come with the territory.
- It's cybersex, so old-fashioned dating rules don't apply.

#31 ... Never let him—or anyone else— know what you did on spring break (or in Vegas).

For many, spring break is a blur. You know you had a good time, but don't quite remember exactly what kind of good time. In fact, you had such a good time that often, when the old gang gets together, and fond moments are recalled, spring break can yield some of those memories you'd rather not relive—like the time you came out of the bathroom with toilet paper streaming out of your underpants. Or the time you got thrown out of that club after getting caught having sex with a stranger on the third-floor balcony. Or that time you won the wet T-shirt contest after you flashed your top—and bottom—to the crowd.

While all of this may have seemed fun—and funny—at the time, they are stories that will make you cringe not too long after you graduate. Later experiences—like your wild girls' weekend in Vegas, or that rowdy bachelorette party you went to in New York—can have the same regrettable quality. Eventually you realize that these are not necessarily high points but often something quite the opposite—and the fewer people who know about your shenanigans, the better.

People are not always themselves when they hit a party scene while on holiday. Or, should I say, they show that side of themselves that should remain a mystery at all other times. What you did in a sunburned, cocktail-induced moment is no reflection of who you are as a person; just what you're capable of when you really let your hair down, to put it mildly. You are who you are every day of the week—not what happened on a crazy beach resort for a week. Let the past stay there, and

I Can't Believe I Did That! On the way back from spring break, my girlfriends and I stopped off at my aunt's place for the night. As soon as we walked in, she sees me glowing from my week of fun, sun, and sex, and says, "Oh my God, girl, you did the DO when you were down there, didn't you?" I went beet red as my girlfriends proceeded to fill her in on our many alcohol-induced adventures. I was too flabbergasted to say anything, and even more so when I got back and heard that my aunt had told my dad how naughty we'd been. I never dared to ask him just how much dirt she spilled. The mortified look on his face said it all.—Izzy remind yourself that what they don't know can't hurt them—or you.

A final corollary to this never rule: never put your boozy, bikini-clad party pix on your MySpace or Facebook profile. Once those pix are out there, they're out of your control. If you do, when you graduate and go out and try to find a real job, don't be surprised if your prospective employers have checked out said booze + bikini holiday pix and made their own judgment about you. That could be four years of hard course work down the drain like the last dregs of a margarita. And what a shame that would be!

It's simple: Have all the scandalous fun you want on holiday, and then go home and remain tight-lipped and camera-shy about it. Really.

#32 ... Never believe him when he says he didn't cheat if the evidence suggests otherwise.

Secretive phone calls. Long brunette hair in his bathroom when yours is blonde. Not making it to your birthday party, and not having a good excuse as to why he was a no-show. His friend suggesting that your boy may have interests other than you, but he doesn't know any details. A picture of an "ex" in his wallet that he "forgot" to take out. Not contacting you the entire time he goes out of town.

These are just a few of the clues the not-so-faithful will leave, indicating that they may be having sexual relations beyond your relationship. Yet many women fail to see these kinds of clues, or simply don't want to see them. Love is blind, and the need to see things as one would want them to be, rather than as they are, further clouds judgment.

It can be easy to miss some signs that your guy is being unfaithful. But there are definitely some more obvious signs to which you should not turn a blind eye. When you're faced with facts that put him squarely in the horndog camp, it's time to confront him with your evidence that he's getting his game somewhere else. It's what happens next that's critical. If he owns up to his misdeeds right off the bat, what follows should be a conversation about the future of your relationship—whether the cheating is a deal breaker or something you decide to work

I Can't Believe I Did That! I happened to glance at my boyfriend's BlackBerry and noticed that there was a message from a woman asking if he could get away to have some fun that night. What made it so suspicious was that I was leaving the city that day. I confronted him about it, but he claimed that she was just a friend he used to date and was harmless. So in love and so needing him, I wanted to believe him, despite girlfriends telling me not to. But after a while I got to thinking differently, so I set up a fake e-mail address and pretended to be her. He fell for it, stringing me (who he thought was her) along while saying that he needed to get rid of his baggage—meaning me and my baby. While I didn't want to see the obvious the first time around, it was too glaring to ignore this time. I confronted him and then I gave him the boot. I just wish that I had saved myself a lot of time and grief in truly seeing the situation for what it was.—Maddy through together. If, on the other hand, he denies cheating and you know better, you need to start looking for the exit signs.

Some men can be very convincing in their denials, even manipulative, making you feel that you're the one being ludicrous to even suggest that $1 + 1 = 2$. It just isn't as you say it is and he can't believe he's being accused of something so wrong, especially when he's in love with you. Stop! Right here is where you need to remind yourself about what you know he's been up to, regardless of his persuasive appeals. If he's not man enough to admit his hurtful mistake, he's not man enough for you. Period. Because now he's not only a cheater, he's also a liar, and those aren't two habits that just go away. Move on, girl. (And if you're the one who's been cheating—see Never #16.)

#33 ... Never go to a psychic for advice on your love life when you're desperate.

When people are troubled, feeling low, or feel as though their lives are out of control, there are two places they go for guidance and solace: religion and psychics. What makes someone lean toward psychics (and horoscopes and Tarot card readers) is the hope that they'll hear what they want to hear—that everything is going to be okay, that they'll get back together, that they'll end up happily ever after.

Look, no matter how desperate you are, you do know you're paying for this kind of advice and are likely to get what you pay for—often vague, harmless encouragement, just enough to keep you out of the depths of despair . . . which sometimes can be just what the doctor ordered. Usually though, it's the source of false or uninformed hope that can get in the way of the work you need to do to make progress in your life.

Even a skilled psychic is unlikely to be able to help you sort out the complicated issues you really need to deal with during difficult times—the nuts and bolts of real-life decision-making that goes way beyond the kinds of questions you might ask a psychic ("Is he the one?" "Will we get back together?"). And if you find a source that's telling you what you want to hear,

I Can't Believe I Did That! Things were falling apart with my boyfriend, and feeling desperate, I went to a psychic. She told me that I was dealing with a past life issue—that Jim and I were lovers from another lifetime, that we were being reunited in this lifetime, and were dealing with a lot of the issues from our previous selves. I know it sounds wacky, but Jim's own psychic had told each of us separately a similar story a couple of months earlier, so when this new psychic said the same thing, I thought there was something to it. And she seemed to have all of the answers. She said she could do the work to get us on the right track in this life. For $1,000, she could start me on rituals, do some spiritual work, and make me a prayer box for me to work with. Hundreds of dollars later, Jim was still being a jerk and I realized that this wasn't a situation I necessarily wanted to have healed, at least not in this lifetime. I deserved better, and he needed to right his wrongs himself, not have some psychic do it for him. I just wish that I'd had my realization before spending all that money on a psychic!—Colleen you're likely to keep going back to it or believe it over what you know to be true in your heart.

Good psychics do seem to have an unexplainable gift. But even a good psychic is often telling you what you already know or is giving you reassurances he or she senses you need. You have all of the answers right in front of you. Trust the cards *you* have and your ability to play them. Everything will fall into place as meant to be based on what you can do for yourself.

Instead of going to a psychic . . .

- ⬭ Keep a journal. Reading back on your struggles will give you the insight and reassurance you need to move forward.
- ⬭ Throw yourself into volunteer work. Taking attention off yourself and placing it on others in need puts things into perfect perspective.
- ⬭ Use that money to travel somewhere. Getting out and seeing the world is always a good way of being reminded of all that the world has to offer you.

#34 ... Never tell him how much you love your vibrator.

A woman's love affair with her vibrator is a special one. It may have been the "first" to touch her in that oh-so-special way, a fondness made even more heartwarming if it was the first to bring her to orgasm. It may even be the only "lover" who can give her mind-blowing multiple orgasms. And often, it's the only efficient form of climactic quickie sex she's ever known. Ask a guy to give you the same charge under time pressure and it's likely not to be half as good.

It's no wonder that many men are intimidated by this magic wand. After all, how can a man possibly compete with a piece of vibrating plastic or silicone that helps a woman to learn more about her body, get over her issues with sexual pleasuring, and take her to new heights, often for the first time (and more consistently than he can, at that)?

So if you're in love with your vibrator, keep it to yourself. Many men don't want to know how good it is or what it does for you. It will simply make him feel insecure about his own ability to pleasure you. Even though most vibrator users will tell you that a vibrator could never replace the intimacy and sensations that come with making love with a man, most men have trouble buying that. After all, many guys are gadget freaks, and their logic is that if it's technology that offers power and speed, it must be better. You will only make both of you

I Can't Believe I Did That!   I hadn't seen my boyfriend in a couple of weeks and he half-heartedly agreed to get together on Super Bowl Sunday. He felt that he was making a sacrifice in not watching the game with the guys, so he wasn't exactly in a lovey-dovey mood when I tried to snuggle up with him and get sexy during the game. While he didn't push me off, he kept his eyes glued to the tube and basically neglected me. Frustrated, I got up, got my vibrator, planted myself at the opposite end of the couch and starting playing by myself with myself. This got his attention, but he didn't bother to come over and try to get in on the action until halftime, with a "So what are we doing over here?" I shot back with "WE are having a lot more fun than I could ever have with you!" He looked like I had shot him. We got into this huge argument after that and even though the makeup sex was great, to this day he doesn't even like the mention of my vibrator.—Liana unnecessarily miserable if you spill the beans that you have a special thing for your vibrator. So don't.

Never tell him how much you love your vibrator UNLESS . . .

- He's not spending enough time with you. It doesn't hurt for him to know you've found "someone else" if you're feeling neglected.
- You're both avid sex toy fans and you know he loves it just as much as you do.
- He gave it to you and wants you to love it.
- He lets you try it out on him and he feels the love himself.

#35 ... Never dive in on rigorous sex without visiting the ladies' room first.

Women don't listen to their bladders enough. When you gotta go, you should go, even if it means interrupting a passionate moment. If you don't, you may end up needing to take a week or more off from lots of potential passionate moments, down and out with a nasty bladder infection. Furthermore, be sure to go #2 if there's any chance of back-door play. Nothing is sexy about praying for it to be over so you can rush to the bathroom and poop. If you don't take care of business, it'll take care of itself. One of the not oft-mentioned aspects of anal penetration is that people have been known to have a bowel movement upon withdrawal, which definitely kills the mood and any orgasmic bliss.

No matter how badly you want sex, want to feel him in you, want to go at it like there's no tomorrow, taking a time-out is definitely worth it for both of you. Just give him a wink and a smile and do the "peepee" dance all the way to the ladies' room instead of torturing yourself during hardcore thrusting. Bladder and bowels empty, you'll feel more relaxed, friskier, and be better able to get into the moment, release your pelvic muscles, and thoroughly enjoy it instead of worrying about your discomfort all the while. You'll be able to enjoy your sexual response and have an easier time climaxing since you won't be worried about the need to go—or consumed with pain! So if you gotta go, give him the best two-minute oral sex of his life before you excuse yourself to "take care of something" in

I Can't Believe I Did That! My boyfriend and I had had this backpacking trek through Europe planned and had been daydreaming about it for weeks. Actually, what we got the most hung up on was all of the places we were going to have sex, starting with the mile-high club. Once in the air, I really had to pee. But when I got up to go to the bathroom, he took it as a cue to get things started. Not wanting to disappoint, especially with the trip just under way, I didn't tell him that my bladder was about to pop. He mistook my stifled cries of pain as we went at it for passion. The next day I woke up with a bladder infection. I didn't say a word as we started our trek. It wasn't until later that day when he wanted to have sex that he learned about my problem. As soon as he penetrated me, I peed all over him. Needless to say, I spent the rest of that vacation on meds and not on him.—Chelsea the bathroom. He doesn't need to know you have to piss like a racehorse. And since when is it a bad thing to make a guy wait a few minutes for what could turn into the ultimate romp?

Finally, pee soon after sex, too, to prevent bladder infections caused by sweat and other bacteria that make their way into your urethra during sex.

#36 ... Never stalk your ex.

It can be really hard to get over someone, especially if you were desperately in love and already planning the wedding, monogramming towels, and naming your children. When people break up, there is often a period full of intense and numerous phone calls and e-mails as one or the other or both try to sort out what went wrong. There may be dramatic, Hollywood-type moments, where one lover makes a grand gesture in a plea to stay together. Sometimes, after being so intertwined in each other's lives, it can be hard to untangle yourselves and move on. But once this time of adjustment is over, you should be well on your way to enjoying singledom once again. If you find yourself actively obsessing over him, however, as in keeping tabs on him, calling his voice mail just to hear his voice, or looking for every opportunity to "bump" into him, then you start to get into stalker territory, which isn't healthy for either of you.

If you find yourself doing anything that crosses the line of social postbreakup conventions, stop immediately. While everyone can sympathize with the brokenhearted, it becomes a whole different story when the behavior becomes intrusive, inappropriate, or illegal. It's just plain scary.

Stalking him will only allow breaking up to cause you more suffering than it already has. All the repetitive negative thinking that goes on only prolongs your pain and delays finding your positive, happy future. This is the time to dive into healthy ways to process your anger and pain, like exercising or doing volunteer work. Get as far away from him as possible.

I Can't Believe I Did That! When my ex broke up with me for another woman, I became this complete psycho-chick. Not only did I do your classic call-and-hang-up incessantly, but I would drive by his house; I would try to hack into his e-mail; I would write him love letters; I would set up fake e-mail accounts pretending to be other women interested in him. The worst of it was, though, that I would follow him around—to the grocery store, to class, to the gym, on a date. . . . It became so routine that one day I wasn't paying attention and accidentally followed him into the men's locker room at our gym. When he realized that I had been stalking him, he became so freaked that he threatened to hit me with a restraining order. At that point, I realized that I had a problem and decided to see a therapist.—Polly

Surround yourself with people and activities you can get lost in so that you can start to forget why you're having such trouble letting go.

Never stalk your ex UNLESS . . .

- You're wondering what you'd look like in a mug shot.
- You think that getting arrested would be a great way to meet single cops.
- You're hoping a temporary insanity plea will work once you are charged with some sort of crime, followed by a kick-ass book deal.

#37 ... Never date a jerk, even if he's beautiful.

Just as a lot of men like to trot around with the stunning "trophy wife," a lot of women like to have a gorgeous beau whom everyone admires. Many people like being associated with good-looking people, and research has found that one of the reasons for this is that others find us more attractive when we hang around with a beautiful crowd. There's a social status that comes along with being involved with a pretty or handsome partner, which many people can find themselves appreciating more than they do the actual person they're involved with, even when the person's personality turns out not to be so pretty.

Leah had been dating this hot, wealthy guy, Matt, who could treat her like a queen at times, taking her to the best social events with other beautiful people, only to be terrible with her at other times. A concerned friend even sent Leah a book on emotionally abusive males, but Leah saw Matt's handsomeness through her rose-colored glasses, and disregarded the book. When yet another friend saw the book at Leah's apartment and thought that it would help with her own abusive relationship, she and Leah read parts of the book aloud to each other. Leah was amazed at how much it described Matt to a T. The cruel things he did sometimes, and nasty comments he made—like "I can't believe how stupid you are"—finally started to sink in, and suddenly, he wasn't so beautiful anymore.

It can be fun to date a great-looking guy, but the second he becomes a jerk, saying nasty things, disrespecting you in public, or standing you up (just to name a few typical beautiful jerk transgressions), tell him Game Over. Nobody's pretty face or rock-hard body is worth being mistreated—verbally, emotionally, or physically—or worth the ultimate toll on your self-esteem. The sentiment "pretty is as pretty does" couldn't be more true when it comes to dating someone. Nobody needs anybody so desperately that they should put up with a jerk—even a GQ jerk.

#38 … Never drop your girlfriends for your guy.

We've all had that girlfriend, the one who always seems to disappear when she has a boyfriend or significant other. You know the one I'm talking about. She's MIA until the second they're on the rocks or done. Then guess who's calling you, crying on your shoulder, longing for support, wailing that she's doomed to be alone . . . until she finds the next one. After a while, you start to feel used and wonder if it's really worth having a friend who only seeks out your company when she doesn't have a man in her life, wanting you to keep her entertained or comforted until another one comes along.

If you find that you're guilty of being that kind of friend yourself, rethink whether any guy is worth the cost of abandoning your social circle. When you ditch your friends for your Romeo, you're creating a toxic, one-way friendship, and your friends are not obligated to stick around after you've dropped them. If you don't nurture your friendships the way you do your relationship, you may find yourself dumped by everyone the next time you have a breakup, as Tamara found out.

From the moment they met in sophomore year of college, Tamara and Henry were inseparable—studying together, eating together, sleeping together. The only time her friends saw Tamara was if Henry was out of town or at one of the few classes they didn't have together. So when their relationship fell apart in the middle of their senior year, Tamara discovered that she didn't really have anybody. "Henry had been my best friend and he was gone. I was so in need of comfort from friends, but found myself having to first reacquaint myself with the people I'd befriended throughout my time at State. But they didn't really know me anymore and I didn't really know them, and the whole situation was awkward for everyone. I needed my friends, but I hadn't been there for them, so they were incredulous that I had any expectations from them." Adding to her pain, Tamara now feels that she missed out on a huge part of her university experience by not allowing herself to enjoy more private time with her friends. "I don't regret my relationship with Henry, but I wish I had done a better job of balancing everything. I could have had a much more well-rounded, fulfilling coed experience and I'd have a lot more friends today."

Unless you and your guy are on a trip around the world, have just had a baby, or have decided to live on a deserted island, there are no excuses for blowing off your friends. It's an insult and hurts everyone—your friends, you, and even your guy—because having a disproportionate amount of energy invested in your relationship with him can be harmful, too. Sure, relationships are consuming, and some partners are more demanding of your time than others. And sometimes your partner can actually be much better company than your friends are, especially if they're giving you attitude or are mopey that you have someone and they don't.

Still, remember this: Guys come and go, but your good friends are always there for you. Let them know that you value them and are thinking of them. Check in with them regularly. It doesn't even have to be too time-consuming—a short e-mail here, a quick phone call there. Just be sure to make the time for your friends. Setting aside time to catch up and bond is all you have to do to stay connected to your pals. Plan get-togethers that can include both your boyfriend and your friends so there's not such an "us" and "them" feel to your relationships. And make a point of having the occasional girls' night out. It helps nourish those friendships and makes you really appreciate going home to your honey.

#39 ... Never keep your ex's number in your cell phone, phonebook, speed dial, or buddy list.

After you drop his toothbrush in the toilet—oops!—the first thing you should do after a nasty breakup is to get him off your radar. Completely. That means removing his number from your cell phone, getting him off any speed dials, and bumping him off your buddy lists online.

Why this draconian purging? If the relationship and breakup were intense and emotional, it can be hard to wash him out of your hair. For many people, getting rid of all contact info is an important part of healing and finally being able to move on. And if you still have feelings for your ex—good or bad—having that number or buddy user name available at the press of a button makes it all too easy to put off the healing that needs to be done with a call or message.

Even if his contact information is tattooed on your brain, erase it everywhere it is recorded. You don't need it anymore. Don't torture yourself by hoping you do. It's as bad as leaving a pack of cigarettes out if you're trying to quit smoking. How can you get over your awful nicotine craving if what you want is right there in front of you?

"It's like an addiction. I can't stop the impulse to text message him!" Having finally dumped her no-good, emotionally abusive boyfriend for all the right reasons, this confession from

I Can't Believe I Did That!   The summer before my junior year I lost my virginity. It wasn't really a serious relationship but the guy was cute and I was a little hung up on him. For a month after we went back to our respective schools, I debated whether or not to stay in touch. Was it really worth it given he was so far away? Having his number programmed in my cell made it all too easy to finally give in and do it. After a night of drinking with my girlfriends, I decided to call him, only we thought it'd be funny to do it on speaker phone to make it a group effort. I rang him, thinking he'd be delighted to hear from me. Instead, he proceeded to tell me how he got hammered the night before, brought home this fat chick and hooked up with her, then woke up to find that he had shit on the stove. I was completely appalled and realized I didn't know this man I'd slept with at all. I never heard the end of it from my friends.—Mandy

Erica is exactly why you should never keep your ex's particulars programmed into your cell or e-mail. "It's just too easy to get in touch with him—too tempting." Erica admits. "I have to keep myself busy with other things so that I don't fire off notes to him." And this for a guy who was a jerk!

Don't keep his contact info handy UNLESS . . .

- You broke up on perfectly good terms and you know you'll remain friends.
- He's also your business partner, lawyer, accountant, agent, or personal assistant and you still have to work with him—if you can!
- Your breakup was really brutal and you might need it for "evidence."

#40 ... Never break up in public.

This is one of those issues you might want to get straight early on in your relationship—no matter how well it's going. Make it a ground rule or a pact that you'll never argue in public. Alternatively, don't ever say a word about it—just be sure never to allow your breakup to happen in public, regardless of who's doing the dumping.

Breaking up in public compromises your privacy and dignity, as well as your abilities to fully express yourself and figure out what's going on. The more emotionally laden the conversation, the harder the breakup, and the more difficult it is going to be to not cause a scene. No matter how much the dumper might want to avoid it, the dumpee deserves to be treated with respect and to have a place to talk, cry, or scream at the top of his or her lungs in private. No one should be forced to lose their composure in front of strangers.

When someone tries to break up in public, it's usually a good indication that he or she is not able to deal with the uncomfortable reality of the situation, whether it's your fault or his. In cases where your guy is dumping you, he knows that being out in public provides a buffer for not getting into the nitty-gritty of matters, making it difficult to truly get anything out in the open. So if he attempts to pull the plug on your relationship in a public place, calmly refuse to be a part of the conversation. He may be a coward for trying to pull this stunt, but you're still in charge of your own behavior and the guardian of your own dignity. Tell him that until he's ready to sit down with you in the privacy of your home, his home, or the middle of nowhere, you're not talking. Get up and leave if you have to.

I Can't Believe I Did That! My ex was too much of a coward to get together in private to break up with me. Instead, he took me out to dinner, thinking he'd find safety in a public setting. When he dropped the bomb on me, I flipped. I started crying and screaming—I was literally in hysterics. As other diners gawked, I called him every four-letter word in the book, and several other regrettable things. At that point, he looked like he was going to cry. The manager finally saved him by asking us to leave. It was such a low blow to have him end things in that way.—Bennie

Now, with the time you've just bought by refusing to have the conversation in a public place, take yourself by the shoulders and get prepared for it. Vow to be composed, commit to showing yourself the utmost self-respect by *not* going postal, and put your best foot forward. Because now that you have his private, undivided attention, you deserve to have a whole rational conversation about it. Every breakup is a potential learning experience and an opportunity to fix whatever is causing one or both of you distress, but only if you're calm enough to listen and ask good questions.

#41 ... Never have sex with your best friend's ex—or vice versa.

Given that most people meet their life partners through their social network, including friends, church, or work, it can be difficult to find your match in the midst of your crowd without stepping on anyone's toes, even if they are no more than footprints from the past. When you find yourself crushing on a friend's ex or your ex's friend, it's a delicate matter trying to get what you want, but still keep the peace. This is even trickier when it involves a best friend, with emotions and reactions becoming even more heightened when somebody feels double-crossed or offended by a trusted loved one.

Even if you come out and ask your best friend if it's okay with her if you date her ex and she says fine, you can't trust her answer. She may think she's fine with it, but he was her man, after all, and that's bound to cause some complicated feelings to surface once it's really happening. And even if she can't say his name without using an expletive, don't take that as a sign that she's over and done with him. This is often an indication that she's still very emotional about their relationship, despite all appearances of having moved on, and your getting involved with him would probably make *you* a candidate for the four-letter word treatment.

Case in point: Cara had an ugly breakup with her home-town boyfriend just before she graduated from college and moved. Shortly thereafter, Cara's best friend, Linda, took up with Cara's ex for a few months until it petered out. When Cara caught wind of this, it didn't matter to her that it was a meaningless fling between her best friend and her ex; even though she had no feelings for her ex, she couldn't get over the feeling of being betrayed by her friend, who she angrily imagined had been pining for her boyfriend all the while Cara was with him. Cara and Linda didn't speak to each other for five years, and even after patching it up, things were never the same.

Finally, when it comes to *your* ex, even if you're done with him, he may not be over you. Or even if he is over you, he might not be keen on your being with anybody else, especially his best friend. While technically it's none of his business who you see after you break up, it doesn't mean you should be careless with his feelings. It's not all about you and what you want.

There are three people involved in this scenario, and it's just not smart to cross the wires of friendship in this way.

It's important also to remember that people often like to recycle their exes. Sometimes it's not really over—yet—and even if they never plan to be intimately involved with their ex again, just the idea that an ex is there can be comforting. Crazy enough, this is even true of people who have moved on and gotten married. They like the idea of a backup should their marriage not work out. People are also very possessive, even if something, or someone, doesn't "belong" to them anymore. When it comes to exes, few like to share.

I Can't Believe I Did That! I met this guy, Kareem, at a bar. Since my name is so common, he didn't realize that I was his best friend, Lamar's, ex-girlfriend, but I knew exactly who Kareem was once I started talking to him. Only I didn't tell him, thinking that it would be interesting to see how far things could go with this cutie pie. He ended up coming back to my place, and one thing led to another. The next morning I told him about our one degree of separation, thinking that he'd find it funny. He was mortified and so pissed that I hadn't told him upfront. He left immediately and never spoke to me again. He must've said something to my ex, too, because Lamar no longer accepts my phone calls the way he used to after our breakup. I didn't think it was such a big deal, but obviously they did.—Sarah

#42 ... Never tell your date you Googled him.

To "Google" somebody or something has become such a popular worldwide pastime that the word was recently added to the dictionary. People are always Googling anybody and everything in an effort to become more informed, whether it's about a potential employer or employee, a hobby, a book, a celebrity, or somebody they're considering getting involved with. It doesn't matter if it's a blind date, somebody you've met through an online dating site, or a cutie you met at a bookstore or bar who wants to get to know you better, the temptation is there: Google him. Everybody is guilty of it and when they actually admit to it, the excuse never fails to be, "But I bet they Googled me too!"

There's nothing wrong with a little research, especially in this day and age. Just make sure your date never finds out you Googled him—at least until he's your boyfriend and the two of you can laugh about it. Googling someone is borderline stalker behavior. And even if you're doing it out of common sense or harmless curiosity, he might not see it that way and might instead see you as some sort of nosy, unstable, "Single White Female" type. Unless he works for Google, he's going to feel spied on. He's going to want to reveal things about himself at his own pace, when he's comfortable doing so—just as you will want to do.

That's how it used to work before there was a Google. People got to know each other, bit by bit, by revealing information about themselves as time went on. This would tend to set a natural pace in the development of a relationship—the more you'd learn about someone, the more you'd like (or dislike) him and decide (or not) that you wanted to know more. Now, between what we can discover about people by Googling them and the information they may put on display about themselves

AND THAT'S A FACT: A recent dating-service survey revealed that 43 percent of respondents admitted to Googling their dates before going out with them. And 88 percent of those same respondents reported that they didn't mind if their dates did the same thing.

I Can't Believe I Did That!   My dad worked for the local police department and as soon as I started dating in high school, the first thing he'd do is run a background police report on the guy to make sure that he was safe. For years, they always came out clean except for this one guy, Dustin, who had gotten busted for hosting a party while underage. When Dustin and I went out to dinner, the conversation turned to alcohol and parties and I made some mention about the time he got busted. He looked all confused and said, "How'd you know about that?" to which I responded, thinking it'd be better than telling him about my dad's background check, "Oh, I uh Googled you." He excused himself to go to the bathroom and never came back.—Suzie

on MySpace or other social networks, well, there's hardly any mystery left!

Go ahead and Google him, but just to be sure he's not one of America's Most Wanted. Don't use Google to obsess over him. And, of course, don't tell him you Googled him. It *never* happened.

#43 ... Never hook up with brothers or roommates.

While blood is thicker than water, when it comes to men, it is the bond of XY that holds them together in solidarity. It is for this reason that the odds are already stacked against you when you are interested in a guy and his brother, or a guy and his roommate. Whether you've gone for one and are now after the other or are hoping to be tag-teamed, hooking up with men who are close is sure to result in a dating dilemma. When all is said and done, you'll have created an awkward dynamic, with you being the odd "man" out. Rather than continue to rendezvous, be in competition with one another, or fight over you, they are likely to have a silent understanding that they've pledged their loyalty to one another rather than to you. When two men know each other and are actually tight, they are not about to fight to the death over a girl, no matter how sexy, gorgeous, or amazing she is. Even if she could be the best time and best sex in the world, most guys are not going to risk bad blood with their bud for the opposite sex. It's just too complicated.

This leaves you at a dating dead end, as Nikki found out. While she was dating Eli, Nikki got to know his roommate Stephen, whom she actually started to like more. To make a long story short, Nikki dumped Eli for Stephen, but after she and Stephen hooked up once, Stephen told her that it couldn't go any further. They had amazing chemistry together, so Nikki was completely floored. His reasoning? He wouldn't get involved with her because she'd dated Eli. He just didn't want to invite any drama, and his loyalties were to Eli. Nikki just couldn't compete with their friendship. Nor should you try to compete with a friendship between two guys—or willingly become some kind of a wedge between them. In the end you probably won't have anything solid with either one of them and you'll have caused bad feelings all the way around. Not cool.

Instead of hooking up with brothers or roommates . . .

- Fantasize about them.
- Find two guys who don't know each other at all, or who at least aren't tight.

Never hook up with brothers or roommates UNLESS . . .

- It's a one-time deal and you don't plan to have anything to do with either of them ever again.
- The roommate is a girl and you're feeling experimental.

#44 ... Never have sex if you're drunk and feeling queasy.

Alcohol can certainly lubricate the mechanism of social exchange, making getting to know someone a little easier, and even making getting intimate with someone easier, too. When consumed in small amounts, it can increase your libido and decrease sexual inhibitions, which can make sex more fun. Yet when you drink too much, especially to the point of feeling wobbly or nauseous, your libido and sexual performance will certainly be compromised, which is not fun—or sexy.

When overly under the influence, women can have lower arousal levels, and this leads to difficulty with climax. This sucks for both you and your lover, and that's only a taste of what can go wrong.

When you are intoxicated, there is a very real danger that you will neglect to use protection during sex, or will be too

I Can't Believe I Did That!   One night my girlfriend, Flora, and I went out bar crawling and ended up hooking up with these two guys who shared an apartment. I had certainly drunk my fair share that night, but it turns out Flora had drunk her fair share and then some. When I got up the next morning and emerged from my hookup's bedroom, I discovered Flora passed out on the couch, buck naked and sprawled out spread-eagle. As if that wasn't horrifying enough, she happened to be having her period and had totally messed up their white couch. Ew. Before the two guys woke up (who mercifully had also had too much to drink) I had to rouse and dress Flora, and then quick-scrub the couch as best I could. Ever since that night, every time I go out I have to worry about running into those two guys.—Joanie

drunk to do it properly. This can put both you and your partner at risk for pregnancy and/or sexually transmitted infections, including HIV. Furthermore, having sex with someone while they are intoxicated can be construed legally as sexual assault or rape. In almost all cases made public, we hear about a woman pressing sexual assault charges against a male. This is not to say, however, that it can't work the other way, too. No one should be having sex with a partner who's too ill or incapacitated to make intelligent, consensual choices. That's a good rule.

In most cases, sex when you're intoxicated turns out to be unsatisfying, sloppy, and basically pointless. You may make decisions you later regret and/or end up making a fool out of yourself. Think how sexy you'd look throwing up or passing out on your date. That's enough to keep you to a two-drink minimum!

#45 ... Never be too lax about his friendships with females.

In an ideal world, you could totally trust your guy with any of his friends—male or female. But in the real world, even if you trust his feelings about a female friendship being strictly platonic, don't trust that the lady friends in his life necessarily see eye to eye with him on this one.

There are all kinds of reasons his female friendship warrants your attention. In the first and worst-case scenario, she's posing as a good friend but is secretly nursing at least a crush on him, and possibly even a full-blown case of unrequited love-of-my-life. No matter how nice this woman may seem—and she may actually be genuinely friendly to you—deep inside, she's wishing you would go away and your guy would suddenly wake up and realize he loves her.

This type of friendship with this kind of woman doesn't have to be a her-or-me deal breaker for you. If she's just a decent if woefully besotted person, be aware of the dynamic and be sensitive to it for everyone's sake. You may never even have to raise the issue with your guy, unless the sitch changes from a benign crush to painful pining that begins affecting your relationship. In that case, you need to get into a serious dialogue with your fella about how he intends to manage the thing. It's his thing to take care of, after all, and if he refuses to do what he needs to help you feel more comfortable (and to protect his good friend's feelings), well, take that into account as you decide how to proceed in your relationship with him.

If the good friend who's really crazy about your guy turns out to be a vicious, conniving, beau-snatching bitch (and you'll be able to smell that from a mile away), that really does call for a her-or-me deal that he needs to work out. If he can't see the situation for what it is, or refuses to make appropriate decisions about it, run, don't walk, toward the exit sign. This is a relationship in which you will *never* feel secure or comfortable—if not outright jealous (and if that's the case, see Never #17).

The other scenario you need to consider carefully is the like-a-sister friendship. This girl can be really great—someone you might be friends with yourself—but she has a claim on your guy that's unique. She knows him very well, shares a personal bond with him (perhaps they went to college together or worked together for a long time), and she usually has a feeling of protectiveness about her friend that's certainly admirable and understandable, but may be the issue you end up contending with.

She's the friend who will always be judging whether you're "good enough" for your guy or whether you're "right for each other." It may not be her place to make these judgments, but she's making them and likely will share these impressions with him at some point. If you end up on the wrong side of these pronouncements, be prepared to eventually get into it with him over this issue. You may even end up moving on if your guy isn't independent-minded enough to make his own decisions about you—in which case, good riddance.

Monica knows how this goes: "My boyfriend had a couple of close female friends who would constantly make plans with him, despite living two hours away from him and knowing that he probably should've been spending this time on his girlfriend or studies. Our relationship fell apart soon after all of them went camping with a bunch of friends when I was out of town. I'm certain that they spent the evening by the campfire encouraging him to get out of his relationship, because when I returned his whole attitude about our relationship had changed. He began acting cool and distant toward me and eventually announced it wasn't working out. Since when? I always knew it was those 'friends' whispering in his ear about me that doomed our relationship."

Some women aren't so subtle, making it quite obvious that they want your guy even if he doesn't feel the same way. Remember, these friends are not harmless. Julia's boyfriend, Ryan, for example, had a friend who, despite having her own boyfriend, made it very clear that she wanted to sleep with Ryan. She would openly flirt with Ryan in front of Julia. And while Julia knew that Ryan would never act on it and knew that he didn't want her, she still hated that the girl would disrespect her, Ryan, and their relationship by trying constantly to get with him. Julia didn't trust the girl as far as she could spit, even though Ryan didn't see his friend as a threat.

This is a situation where you should make like the mafia: keep your friends close and your enemies closer. Be impossibly friendly, and go through all the motions of cheerful acquaintance. Invite her for a girls' night out. Be around when you know she will be, too, so she's always in your scopes. After a while, you will either convince her with your faux friendly intentions and she'll lay off your guy, or you will freak her out with your Stepfordly attentions and she'll lay off because she's scared of you. Either way, problem solved!

#46 ... Never answer your phone during sex.

Thanks to cell phone technology, we can pretty much talk on the phone anywhere, anytime. But just because we can, doesn't mean we should—especially when having sex.

A passionate encounter is definitely one of those times—like being on an airplane, in church, or at the movies—when a strict cell-phones-off policy is called for. Why? Okay, good manners, for starters. Sex is a unique and private moment between two people, each of whom deserves the other's undivided attention. Anyone who purposely leaves on their cell—or worse, answers it—during sex is rude and unworthy of your intimate company. Besides that, it's a passion killer, a pause in the momentum that can rarely be recaptured.

Answering the phone during sex sends a message to your partner that you're not really present in the moment or that you're not interested or satisfied enough by it to focus on it. Think about how bummed your partner would feel to discover

that you cared more about taking a call than pursuing your mutual pleasure. How would you feel if he did the same?

Christa found out just how offensive it could be when her college boyfriend answered the phone while she was going down on him. His friend must've asked what he was doing because Christa heard him respond, "Nothing." He was lucky that she didn't castrate him right then and there. Christa was furious that (a) he could be rude enough to answer the phone, and (b) that he couldn't at least say something like, "Christa and I are having the most amazing time, so can I call you back?" It totally ruined the mood of what had started out as a really hot time.

People can be rude in general when it comes to their cell phones—talking too loud, using them at inappropriate times and places, or constantly checking for calls instead of concentrating on the conversation with you. So don't be surprised to encounter the ultimate rude cell phone behavior of answering during sex from time to time. When it happens, you can throw his cell phone at his head and storm out, give him one last chance to never do it again, or, most effective, announce your cell-phones-off rule before you even begin fooling around.

#47 ... Never tell your friend you don't like her partner/fiancé.

You don't have to like everyone. But there are times when you need to tolerate a certain someone, whether it's a family member, somebody marrying into your family, a roommate's sweetie, or a friend's partner. Such situations are tough because you're regularly thrown in close social quarters with someone who's not your cup of tea. So when one of your good chums falls in love with somebody you don't care for, it can make for some strained relations and get-togethers, as well as aggravating girl-talk powwows about men, love, and lust. You're sitting there biting your tongue because you know your thumbs-down opinion is unlikely to change the situation for the better. If anything, it will only get worse.

Rule of thumb: A woman will always pick her partner over her girlfriend. She may come back to you later, yes, but if push comes to shove, she'll tell you to get lost before she gives him the boot, especially just because you don't like him. So if you want to keep her as a friend, you need to come to terms with the fact that even though you don't like him, she does. You need to find a constructive way to deal with your negative feelings and ways that the two of you can still be friends, perhaps without your being subjected to his company quite as much. As her friend, your opinion is valued—and that's why it's going to become hurtful and destructive if you let her know that you don't care for her Prince Charming. People are very protective of their partners and do not like to hear them being criticized (unless they are voicing their own personal gripes).

So you need to accept that there's something about this guy that turns her on, makes her smile, tugs at her heartstrings—you may not see it, but she does. Even if you don't care for this person, he makes her happy, and that's what's most important.

Never tell your friend you don't like her partner/fiancé UNLESS . . .

- Your negative feelings about him are proven by some caddish behavior you observe firsthand—like he hits on you when she's out of town.
- You see that he's hurting or abusing her. In that case, you have to speak up out of friendship.

#48 ... Never take advice from just anyone about sex.

All of us are "sexperts." We are sexual human beings, from the time we are born until the day we die. We all have our own experiences, opinions, and knowledge about sex, and we all think we have something to say about it. Yet, unfortunately for the field of sexology, and for sex experts who are actually educated and trained, lots of people claim authority that they don't really have on the subject. Just because a person has had a lot of sex doesn't make him or her an expert on the subject. So when your friends are weighing in on this or that about sex, do take it with a grain of salt. Lots of grains. And even if someone has a sex column or blog or even a book, if this "sexpert" doesn't have any expertise behind his or her claims, or is insensitive about how information is delivered, beware the accuracy of what is said. Think of it like this: If you needed medical advice, would you turn to somebody who doesn't have an M.D., N.P., or R.N. following their name? If you were seeking psychological help, wouldn't you prefer getting it from somebody who has undergone years of training in psychology or therapy? Anybody can have an opinion on sex. Given a pulpit, many will tell you all about it. This does not make them experts.

So don't shortchange yourself when it comes to sex advice. Make sure that you scrutinize your resources and determine if they're legit, as Miranda found that she needed to when she read an article on fantasies: "It was in a popular men's magazine, and this psychiatrist was answering some guy's question on whether fantasizing about women other than his wife was okay. The doc basically told him that it was wrong and that he should make a concerted effort to stop doing so. This didn't sound right to me, and sure enough, a sexologist friend of mine confirmed that there was nothing wrong with fantasizing about other people during sex—that, in fact, it has been found to help couples stay monogamous."

Even sources that seem credible may not be, with certain professionals lacking training specifically in sexuality or speaking from another generation's outdated ideas about sex. Furthermore, many people, even experts, are in the media because they can pay people to have you listen to them—not because they are the most noteworthy in their field. They don't always have your best interests at heart, but rather their own need for publicity and attention. So don't be a passive receiver of information, letting just any "expert" dictate your values, behaviors, and attitudes when it comes to sex—do your homework, own your sexual learning, and figure it out for yourself!

#49 ... Never check his e-mail "just to see what he's been up to."

Don't check his e-mail—or his voice-mail or his regular mail for that matter. And stay away from his PDA, while you're at it. Such things are private and important personal boundaries to respect, between casual daters and long-marrieds alike. Being a couple does not entitle you to violate your partner's privacy and to breach his trust by not minding your own business. Even if you think it is no big deal or don't expect that it will do any harm, you may come to regret it.

Here's why: Once you go down that road it's hard to turn back. The snooping will become a nasty habit and you'll find yourself in a constant state of suspicion—even if he hasn't done anything to be suspicious about! The worst part is that you're breaking the bond of trust for both of you. Trust is a two-way street and is both a benefit and a requirement of every good relationship. If you don't have it, you pretty much don't have anything. So why would you squander it by unwarranted snooping?

If you want to know what he's "up to," ask him. If he's behaving in a way that makes you suspicious, don't sneak around and spy on his stuff. Be direct and ask him. And if you think he's lying, he probably is. In which case, you know what to do!

#50 ... Never ask him if you look fat.

Most men will wholeheartedly back this particular "never"—they can't stand the question! It puts your tough guy in an impossibly tough situation which, if he's like most other males, he doesn't handle well. It's a classic damned if you do, damned if you don't dilemma for him. Whether he answers honestly or lies, you are likely to fault him for both answers. Either response is suspect, and he's made to feel awful and unsupportive, despite not having done a thing except answer the question *you* asked him. Ultimately, he just feels frustrated by his powerlessness to please you with an answer, and you feel miserable because no answer satisfies you.

Perhaps the most important reason you should never ask him this question is that it lets him know that inside, you're feeling insecure—and that is so *not* sexy. Half of what makes him think you're hot is that you think you're hot. Confidence and healthy self-image is a huge turn-on for everybody. And self-doubt and a negative self-image—as evidenced by that stupid question—are not.

Asking him if you look fat only highlights your body image issues, putting them out there as a ridiculous, unnecessary subject of discussion. Just think of it the other way around. If he was busy asking you about his weight, his cellulite, his butt being too big, wouldn't it be a total turn-off to you?

Tyra remembers one ex who had been on the cross-country team in college and had always been stick-skinny. After graduation, he gained weight because he wasn't running all the time anymore. Tyra thought he looked great, but whenever he would fret about his butt or midsection getting big, she

I Can't Believe I Did That! I had been working out all summer, namely running and lifting weights. I could tell that I was becoming more toned and slimming down, so I asked my boyfriend if I was fat, expecting him to say, "No way, babe. You look amazing! Your hard work is really paying off." Instead, his response was, "Well, let's just say it's a good thing you're working out. Your butt and thighs seem to have gotten a bit thicker lately." I wanted to strangle him, and felt the sudden need to insult his football player body with, "Oh yeah, well you have man boobs!" He didn't speak to me for a week.—Sophia

wondered if he was seeing something she didn't. It was a total turnoff and Tyra finally understood why men can't stand it when women are so critical of themselves.

Asking for somebody's reassurance that you look good, especially if it's done on a regular basis, gets old really fast and is unappealing. If your guy is with you, is in love with you, and clearly enjoys being intimate with you, then that's the only answer you need about how he feels about you—and your weight.

#51 ... Never fall for the line, "I feel a connection between us."

Or any of the following:

"Your father must've been a thief—because he stole the stars from the sky and put them in your eyes."

"Do you believe in love at first sight?"

"I lost my phone number—can I have yours?"

"You must be tired because you've been running through my mind since the last time I saw you here."

"I hope you know CPR because you take my breath away!"

"I've just moved you to the top of my 'to do' list."

"If you don't want to have kids with me, then why don't we just practice?"

"Screw me if I am wrong, but haven't we met before?"

"That dress would look great in a crumpled heap next to my bed."

"Were you arrested earlier? It must be illegal to look so good."

"The only thing you haven't told me is your name."

"How should I cook your eggs for breakfast?"

"I must be in heaven! Because you're an angel."

"Apart from being sexy, what do you do for a living?"

"Do you know karate? 'Cuz your body is really kickin'."

"Excuse me. I'm from the FBI, Fine Body Investigators, and I'm going to have to ask you to assume the position."

Those are just a handful of the pickup lines out there that you should never fall for no matter how much you long for a man's attention or want to get laid. Some men will do and say anything to get you into bed, with some players being much better at this type of seduction than others. It's a total game to these smooth operators. There are Web sites dedicated entirely to pickup lines that help men approach and meet women with no rejection, and get her in the sack, too.

Sure, there are some sweet guys out there lamely using these lines who may really be worth getting to know a little better. There also are cheesy men who make your skin crawl before the line is even out of their mouths—you know it's coming and it's easy to deflect. But the ones who are the most dangerous—and successful—are those who know how to give a good performance, as Adele describes: "One happy hour, I met this gorgeous Persian attorney, who was the friend of a friend. He bought me a drink and then another, but, having had a very painful breakup recently, I could not enjoy the attention he was pouring on me and I had to get away from him and all the pressure he was putting on me to play the feisty repartee game. A couple of months later, at our mutual friend's wedding reception, he was giving me all these wonderful compliments. In a better space emotionally, I found myself wondering if maybe I could dig this guy—only for him to ruin things with, "I feel a connection between us—and I have since the first time we met." I remembered all too well my drunken, mournful state when we met and how sloppy and unattractive I had been, so I told him I wasn't buying it. A couple of minutes later, I spotted him chasing after a bridesmaid. Big surprise."

#52 ... Never date a guy who won't introduce you to his friends.

Being introduced to his friends is usually a pretty good sign that he is into you and the idea of the two of you. It's a pretty serious step for a guy, with meeting the family the next major indicator that this relationship is for real. So if he doesn't invite you to gatherings with his friends or doesn't acknowledge you when they're around or doesn't show any interest in having you get to know them, then it's usually a pretty good sign that he doesn't see your relationship as an important part of his whole circle of friendships. This could be a reflection of a lot of things—trouble with commitment, peer pressure not to get into a serious relationship, or even a basic lack of maturity or social skills. These may or may not be issues you can do anything about.

Worst-case scenario, the reason he's not letting you meet his friends is that he's got a whole other life going, complete with other girlfriends that he needs not to know about *you*, too! Or it could be that his friends *are* girls who maybe aren't so keen on his romantic lady friends.

Whatever the reason, you have to ask him what's up. Listen to what he says and how he says it. If he's evasive or cagey, you might just be looking at the worst-case scenario. If he just looks a little pained or uncomfortable, gently encourage him to share his reasoning with you.

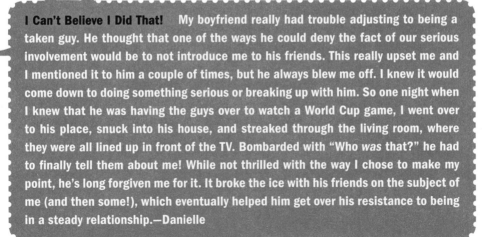

I Can't Believe I Did That!   My boyfriend really had trouble adjusting to being a taken guy. He thought that one of the ways he could deny the fact of our serious involvement would be to not introduce me to his friends. This really upset me and I mentioned it to him a couple of times, but he always blew me off. I knew it would come down to doing something serious or breaking up with him. So one night when I knew that he was having the guys over to watch a World Cup game, I went over to his place, snuck into his house, and streaked through the living room, where they were all lined up in front of the TV. Bombarded with "Who *was* that?" he had to finally tell them about me! While not thrilled with the way I chose to make my point, he's long forgiven me for it. It broke the ice with his friends on the subject of me (and then some!), which eventually helped him get over his resistance to being in a steady relationship.—Danielle

If you're crazy about him and he's crazy about you, he may be ready to make some changes or grow up a little in order to pursue a relationship with you. If you think that may be the case, don't try to force him to take dramatic measures, like throwing a big party for you to introduce you to his friends. Instead, take it slow, perhaps meeting them one by one as your guy feels comfortable making the connections among you. Just keep in mind that this is something you both want, and the more you can help him make these adjustments in ways that are true to his nature and personality, the more likely all will turn out well.

Here's the flip side of that scenario: He really doesn't want to let you into his life and he's happy enjoying a little "action" with you that doesn't interfere with his other friendships or pastimes. He will make this abundantly clear by never allowing your path to cross with his buddies! You probably will not be invited to meet his family, either. This is a classic compartmentalizer you're dealing with—he keeps you in one place and the rest of his life in another—so your situation is never going to get any better than this. Unless this is what you want out of the relationship, too, grab your toothbrush and move on.

#53 ... Never send e-mail that includes details of your latest sexual exploits to a coworker.

Mixing your business and personal life is never advisable. Even if people at work are your friends, they are also your colleagues, and you do have a professional relationship first and foremost. In some cases, this relationship can be a competitive one, so the fewer people in the workplace who know about your personal life, the better. It's a matter of not knowing whether something will come back to haunt you, or information about your wrongdoings will fall into the wrong hands, or you'll be all-out backstabbed by someone you thought you could trust when it comes to workplace power plays.

This really is a basic never rule that is perhaps especially hard to adhere to if you have good friendships among coworkers. Why *shouldn't* you share stories with friends about your social life, or share juicy details of your latest hot date the next morning by e-mail? The reason is simple: That kind of information is by definition private, and every single time you choose to share it, electronically or otherwise, you make yourself vulnerable to idle gossip at best, and vicious rumor at worst.

Furthermore, office gossip is brutal. Your coworkers don't have to wait for the office Christmas party to get you into

I Can't Believe I Did That! I hated my job, partly because one of my coworkers was my boss's daughter, Nancy. She was lazy and intolerable and obviously worked there because she was daddy's little girl. I would be nice to her, with gritted teeth, while everyone else would kiss her butt because of her family ties. In true, nepotistic fashion, when the opportunity for a promotion came along, I was passed over so that she could advance, despite the fact that I was more experienced and outqualified her in every way. Feeling unappreciated, I looked for another job and got one. But before I left my old job, fate gave me an opportunity for revenge. My e-mail address was only one letter off from another employee's—Nancy's best friend, who also got her job by association. Nancy had accidentally sent me an e-mail, detailing all of the dirty things they'd both done with a man they'd met at a bar the night before in the club's bathroom. Before I closed out my work e-mail for the last time, I decided that I wasn't the only one who should get to enjoy their skank adventures, so I forwarded the e-mail to none other than my boss, making sure to "bcc" everyone in the office as well.—Rachel trouble. Why do that when the office rumor mill is alive and well via e-mail, especially if you were the foolish instigator, sending details of your sexploits to someone you thought you could trust?

When you offer up even the tiniest tidbit of personal info about yourself, you open the door—yourself, by choice—to a whole range of nasty repercussions no longer in your control. What if some jealous coworker gets her hands on one of your racy e-mail tales and "accidentally" forwards it to your boss? Or to your mother? Or to your boyfriend? Most scandals are initiated by none other than the subjects of the scandals—because they just couldn't keep their mouths shut about their private affairs or showed fatally poor judgment about those with whom they shared these details. Enter the electronic age, and the possibility of your private exploits gleefully being shared with the whole world through forwarded e-mail. That *could* happen to you, and it would all be due to foolish blabbermouthed indiscretion you could have avoided just by not hitting the "send" button.

#54 ... Never get involved with him if he still lives with his parents, ex-wife, ex-girlfriend, or college buddies.

Sometimes you can be falling for the most amazing guy in the world until the strangest thing puts the whammy on your relationship—he invites you to his home. As it slowly dawns on you what he meant exactly by "his place," little red flags go up and whistles start going off in your head. Yes, that's Mom he's asking if she's finished his laundry yet. Or indeed that's his college roommate of ten years in the living room, watching porn while scarfing nachos and a beer. And was that his ex in a satin bathrobe you brushed past in the kitchen, who's now "just" an apartment mate who shares a bathroom?

While every circumstance is unique, there are certain general rules that apply in certain living situations in which you may find him dwelling. If he's still living with a former partner, it's either not totally over or too complicated of an arrangement to simply pull the plug on (they share a lease, a mortgage, or ownership of a dog). These complications may be understandable, but it doesn't mean they're acceptable. Sure, sometimes people get trapped in sharing the same roof over their heads for financial reasons, but when he has a tent pitched in the backyard or refers to his best bud's pull-out couch as his crib, you're better off forgetting about him.

If he's still not only living with his college buddies, but also still living up the frat boy lifestyle, he's likely not going to tire of any of the things they've enjoyed since college anytime soon, namely parties, women, and booze. He probably still has some oats left to sow and isn't looking to get seriously involved anytime in the near future. So unless you're up for something strictly casual—and much more like life was in high school or college—stay away from this guy.

Last, if he's still living with his parents, then he probably has some issues that he needs to deal with before he can be in a mature, adult relationship. Sure, there are times when people need to fall back on their parents and move back into their old room, such as when unexpectedly unemployed or during a life transition. But stays like that should only be temporary. If he doesn't have a plan to be out of mom and pop's bed-and-breakfast anytime soon, make sure you don't plan anything long-term with him.

Diana, for example, knows all too well why this situation is not worth the issues involved. When her boyfriend arrived back from having been deployed overseas, Diana couldn't wait to start the next phase of their relationship. She moved to his hometown so that they could be closer, thinking that in a couple of months, he'd have a job and be on his own and that they'd be ready to start their life together. But things swiftly went downhill once he was again living under his parents' roof. He got really comfy not having to pay bills, so he was completely unmotivated to look for a job. With his mom doing the cooking, cleaning, and laundry, he loved the live-in maid service. With the government paying for some medical problems related to his time in the service, he had some money coming in, which made him even lazier when thinking about his and Diana's future. The clincher: His family was Catholic, so out of respect for his parents he'd never spend the night at Diana's place, even though he was thirty years old! No surprise, his mother despised Diana, making it really uncomfortable for her to go over and visit him. So before the relationship even got off the ground, it was over.

> **AND THAT'S A FACT:** According to the United States Census Bureau, 25 percent of adults aged eighteen to thirty-four, or nearly 18 million people, live with their parents. This means that if you date within this age group, there's a 1-in-4 chance he's sleeping in his childhood bed tonight.

If your date, crush, or boyfriend is in any of these dependent living situations, don't proceed any further unless you're ready to deal with all of the extra baggage that comes along with this territory. In fact, telling him that the two of you aren't going to happen until he's a bit more independent may motivate him to become just that—if he likes you enough. If not, throw him back and find somebody who is in a much better place—domestically and emotionally—to give you what you want.

#55 ... Never talk about things your previous lovers did in bed.

For the most part, people hate hearing about their partner's former lovers. And what they despise even more is hearing about intimate, skin-on-skin moments with those lovers. It can be excruciating to know how incredible this move was, or how sweet and sensual this touch was, or how you'd never experienced "seX, Y, and Z" before—or since. Even if your ex deserves to be world renowned as the Muhammad Ali of rear entry, cunnilingus, or tantric sex, don't ever mention to your current date, crush, or partner what he did, how he did it, or how well he did it. Noting a former lover's prowess will only create performance anxiety and unnecessary concern.

Your current guy will feel pressure to perform against the measure of your former superlover every time he's intimate with you, not only hyperaware of his every move, but wondering if you are, too. He'll be concentrating more on whether he's doing it as well as your former lover and less on the mutual pleasure of the whole experience. If he's no longer feeling sexually confident when he's in between the sheets with you, you will ultimately suffer the consequences of your big mouth, when your own pleasure is compromised.

Instead of blabbing about your previous sexploits, here's an idea: take what you learned from your super-duper ex-lover and ever-so-subtly, without *saying* a word, share this valuable sexual wisdom with your new man. Of a lifetime of sexual relationships, this is definitely the best kind—where you share something wonderful you have experienced in a way that expands the experience of your partner, and likely improves both of your experiences as you move on to future relationships. Oh, and it feels pretty sweet in the here and now, too!

It's not just the hot-hot-hot sex memories you should keep to yourself. It's *all* of them. Don't tell him the who or where or how about any of your previous experiences. Knowing you're already a member of the mile-high club, for instance, may discourage him from wanting to play that game with you himself. And that would be a bummer, no?

So forget about going on and on about your hot ex-lovers and your sexual history and focus on seeing your current love become your next hot ex-lover! Or better yet, watch him become a sensational lover and then keep him!

Instead of talking about things your previous lovers did in bed . . .

- ○ Love the one you're with. That means focus your attention on the unique and wonderful qualities—sexual and other-wise—of the man who currently makes your heart sing.
- ○ Save your special sexual memories of Mr. Ex for private moments when you're going it alone. That's a healthy, sexy, constructive way to put your experience to good use!

#56 ... Never date a guy who's more concerned about his hair than you are about yours.

If a man you're dating is consumed with his hair, clothes, shoes—basically anything appearance-related—more than you are with your own, run the other way! These habits are usually a good indication that he's totally into himself and conceited, or that he's insecure and overly worried about keeping up appearances—or a bizarre combination of the two. Not only is this completely unattractive, but it boils down to less time that he's going to spend doting on you. He'll be too busy with himself! He may even try to upstage you at times, wanting people to look at him instead of the babelicious bombshell on his arm.

Look, it's one thing for a man to want to be well-groomed and look good, especially if he's on a date and wants to impress you. But you can usually sniff out the ones who are super high-maintenance—quite literally. Dead giveaways are lots of cologne, hair that's perfectly set and shiny, blinding white teeth, a bronze-orange tan, and more trips to the loo than someone with a case of diarrhea. Note that metrosexuals don't necessarily fit into this category. While some may criticize it, there's nothing wrong with a man who likes to be well-manicured

I Can't Believe I Did That!   Despite projecting this hippy-type image, complete with a rumpled, slightly disheveled look, my ex-boyfriend was obsessed with his long locks. He was so proud of his hair and was convinced that it made an important statement about him. He would spend up to two hours in the bathroom, working on his hair and his carefully orchestrated unkempt look. It was unreal and annoying, especially since I had long hair, too, and would hardly give it a thought when it came to maintenance. So I would have to wait around for him a lot and we were always late for events. Anyway, as our relationship took a nosedive, he got more and more critical of me—my looks, my laugh, my figure, my interests, my statements. I guess he was so perfect in comparison, or so he thought. The straw that finally broke the camel's back was when he made some nasty crack about my hair before flouncing his mane over the arm of the couch and dozing off. Seething, I grabbed a pair of scissors, and though I was tempted to pull a Delilah and cut off all his hair, I did give it a helluva hack job before leaving him once and for all.—Pam and well-groomed. However, unless his name is RuPaul, a guy who's too into his personal grooming behaviors has much larger issues, which you're better off not subjecting yourself to.

So after you've gotten to know the slicked-up, best-dressed version of your man, you should begin to see what the rumpled, underdressed side of him is like—the equivalent of you in your sweats and slippies. If he's careful never to let you see that side of him, it could be because there *isn't* that side of him—and do you really think you're up to being involved with Beau Brummell?

#57 … Never have more to drink on a first date than he does.

There's a great Icelandic word that gets a colorful reaction anytime an Icelander hears it. That eyebrow-raising word is *drusla*. A drusla can be a lot of things, and almost any woman can be a drusla without trying too hard. All she has to do is dress a little provocatively if fashionably, sleep around (or at least give the impression that she does), throw herself at men, smoke like a fiend, and enjoy getting plastered on a fairly regular basis.

Though those aren't very desirable descriptors, everyone in Iceland seems to love a good drusla. She's a lot of fun, makes for good gossip, is lovable, and is always up for having lots of cocktails and socializing. So if you want to be a drusla, especially if you're visiting Iceland, make sure you not only drink on a first date, but that you get hammered. Otherwise, show

> **AND THAT'S A FACT:** Compared to men, women have less body fluid and a higher percentage of body fat. Because alcohol is not readily absorbed into fat, a woman will have a higher blood alcohol concentration than a man of the same weight who drinks the same amount of alcohol as she; the woman will also feel the effects of the alcohol for a longer period of time.

some restraint on your first date and throughout the getting-to-know-you stage—you won't regret it.

While it can be impressive (in a *Guinness Book of World Records* kind of way) to keep up with your date drink for drink, it is simply unwise to try to outdrink him. Partly, this is biological; it takes a woman's body twice the time it does for a man's body to process the same amount of alcohol. This is because women have a smaller quantity of alcohol dehydrogenase, which is the enzyme needed to break down alcohol, and because women tend to be smaller than men, meaning their blood alcohol content is higher despite drinking the same amount.

So if getting drunk together is your game, add up all those shot glasses, beer bottles, or margarita mugs in front of you and divide by two to understand how definitively you lose your competitive edge. From a strictly physical standpoint, this is one game you will not win.

More important, though, getting more trashed than your date is begging for trouble. Besides simply making a spectacle of yourself, you also increase your chances of having unprotected or, even worse, unwanted sex. The idea is to be your best, most in-control self when getting to know someone, not your most soused and sloppy self! So no matter how much he eggs you on to "keep up" or have "just one more," stay in charge of yourself—your first impression, your reputation, even your own safety—by moderating your alcohol consumption. If he can't handle your restraint, he should be headed for the curb anyway. If he respects your behavior, well, maybe you'll just decide to see him for a second date!

#58 ... Never get involved with a guy who's not as smart as you are.

Single, educated women who have been out on the dating scene for a while, especially those who are MDs or PhDs, will tell you in a heartbeat not to waste your time by committing this never. A man can think you're the greatest thing since sliced bread, and adore the fact that you're brilliant, that you have good common sense, that you're witty, that he can have amazing conversations with you, that you have the IQ of Einstein, that he can learn so much from you . . . and still dump you simply for being too smart, or at least smarter than he is. So rather than even give the not-so-smart guys a chance, it's usually better just to avoid them entirely.

Take Elise, for example, a beautiful, sexy woman, with everything to offer, who has learned the hard way that while men can appreciate her intellect and PhD, they'll ultimately hold them against her: "I've dated TV producers, investment brokers, writers, trust fund babies, even a male stripper, and they've all expressed concern about my intellectual level and schooling when they've broken things off with me. There was nothing wrong with our relationship dynamics at all—we had plenty of fun together and good chemistry. But it bugged the hell out of them that I was so 'overeducated,' as one guy put it. They couldn't explain their problem, but I always got the feeling they thought I was 'slumming,' intellectually speaking."

There's a difference between being educated and being smart, of course, and it's the smartness that other smart people find attractive in you—and you in them. Which is why the challenge in dating someone who's not as smart as you is usually more your problem than his. He may be intimidated by your intellect but he's also probably attracted to it. Smart is

AND THAT'S A FACT: It's only going to get harder to meet guys who are as smart as you are. Statistics show that men are less likely than women to get bachelor's degrees—and when they do, their grades aren't as good as women's. It turns out women are on a fast and fierce pace to out-achieve their male counterparts in academia, and the ultimate consequence will be that women will have fewer prospects to consider among men as educated as they are!

sexy, after all. Intellectually stimulating is even sexier. Not so smart, on the other hand, isn't that sexy. In fact, eventually it is likely to get on your nerves. You'll try not to notice it, you'll remind yourself of how sweet or sultry he is, you'll think about how lucky all your friends think you are for having this sweet, hot boyfriend. But in the end, it will bug you that he doesn't know or care to know about some of the more sophisticated subjects that rock your boat—which will leave you rocking your own brainy boat all by yourself. That's not sexy, either.

Instead of getting involved with a guy who's not as smart as you are . . .

- Try to work in a field where there are a lot of smart guys— medicine or law or academia. Hey, you're smart, you should be doing that anyway!
- Limit your not-so-smart-guy dalliances to hot one-nighters. Just because he can't spell doesn't mean the tumble won't be worth your while!

#59 ... Never engage in sex play unless you really feel playful.

Sex is everywhere, and the Internet, media, and alternative communities seem to be egging us on to have all kinds of sex just because we can. Our pornified culture constantly taunts us to quit being so "square," to be more sexually liberated. In light of such messaging, many people come away with the idea that to be sexually free means that you have tried it all, bared it all—even when you didn't really want to.

Know that simply making an exhibitionist out of yourself or being willing to do everything and anything with anybody and everybody does not necessarily make you sexually in charge of yourself. Instead, sexual freedom is about being able to explore your sexuality and desire within your own comfort zone, by getting to know yourself, your pleasures, your limits, and what intimacy means to you. It's about not engaging in sex play when you don't want to. You're in charge of your body; you call the shots when it comes to your sexuality. Don't let anyone make you feel otherwise.

No matter what you do, make sure that you're looking after and satisfying yourself. If you're not in the mood, then you're not in the mood—no excuses. You don't have to apologize for being tired, stressed, hungry, too sick, or not interested in the present opportunity. Make sure you're staying true to yourself and your values—that you're listening to your mind, body, and soul before engaging in any sex act with anybody. If you don't, you may end up doing something you regret. Also, if you're not into it or the moment, then you're likely to compromise

I Can't Believe I Did That! It was my last semester in college, at a university with quite a sex reputation, and I was at a party where some people were drinking, some doing drugs. Determined to live it up before graduation, and completely high, I couldn't turn down the opportunity to have a threesome, which soon turned into an orgy. I had more sex than I can remember, probably with six or seven people—and the worst part was that it was totally unprotected. While I didn't, thankfully, end up with any STDs that I know of, I did end up getting pregnant—and I had no clue who the father was.—Lauralei your sexual response, making the experience all the less plea-surable for you and your lover.

Instead of engaging in sex play . . .

○ Make a date with yourself or your lover for another time, when you're likelier to be more turned on.
○ Cuddle.
○ Do what you'd rather do instead!

#60 ... Never send him dirty text messages while he's at work.

Text messaging (TMing) has become a favorite way for lovers to get each other all worked up with throughout-the-day foreplay. Why take the time to write old-fashioned love letters when you can shoot off a 15-to-30-letter message that professes your love or describes your throbbing loin or makes your sweetie feel desirable or gives tantalizing hints of what's to come?

TMing is a handy tool to let your beloved know you're thinking of him. Yet there are times when you should think twice about TMing your love, specifically when he's at work. While amusing and fun, TMing can be very distracting, keeping him from his responsibilities or from paying attention to the business meeting he's in. Furthermore, have a heart. Don't give him a hard-on at the office. Some of your TMs are going to do just that, making it impossible for him to stand up and give that presentation to his boss and colleagues. He'll be sweating bricks fighting his erection and if someone catches on to his dilemma, he'll feel like a fool.

Unless he's *begging* you to keep him entertained with saucy TMs throughout the day or you know for a fact he's alone, don't engage in provocative TMing. Keep it PG-rated and save the XXX TMs for when he's on his way home—to you.

#61 ... Never divulge all of your fantasies.

Fantasies can be hot—so hot it's not unusual to want to share them. After all, a pleasure shared is pleasure doubled. In the case of fantasies, however, it's often hotter if you keep at least a few to yourself. Your fantasies help you to get aroused, help you stay monogamous in your relationship, and help spice things up sometimes. Sharing fantasies can foil some of the benefits of having your own private little X-rated theater between your ears. Giving them away can disempower them, especially if you don't get the reaction you're hoping for.

Another reason to keep some fantasies to yourself is that your partner may not like what he hears, or may even feel threatened by your vixenish visions. While some guys may totally get off on hearing that you fantasize about threesomes, group sex, other women, bondage, or being caught on camera, some may get turned off to you entirely. Others may actually put pressure on you to live out your fantasy, even if it's

> **AND THAT'S A FACT:** Studies have shown that female sexual fantasies are distinctly different from male sexual fantasies in a few key ways. First, female fantasies tend to contain familiar partners—guys they currently are, have been, or want to be romantically or sexually involved with. Guys fantasize more often about strangers or unattainable Penthouse Pet types. Women tend to fantasize in a very detailed context (what she's wearing, where it takes place, what is said), whereas men's fantasies tend to be much more nonspecific. Along with the sexual component, female fantasies tend to have an emotional component, including love, affection, and even commitment, whereas male fantasies tend to be strictly sexual. Women often fantasize about their own attractiveness to men and/or about being submissive, where men just don't. In short, a woman's fantasy is more likely to be a whole story starring her, complete with costumes, exotic settings, sexy dialogue, and deeply passionate feelings. A man's fantasy is more likely to be a short scene involving him, Jenna Jameson, and his orgasm.

not your true libidinal longing when faced with the actual opportunity.

Everyone has different standards as far as what they find sexy. It's always good to have a few fantasies up your sleeve in case your lover is having an off day in bed or if you're not exactly in the mood. Having those special private fantasies to fall back on can give you the charge you need to get turned on and/or attain orgasm. If you spill all your beans about it, a fantasy can lose its thrill, especially if you end up acting it out, only to discover that it's not all that. Some things are better left to the imagination, so be careful to share your fantasies with your partner with discretion.

That said, don't be afraid to indulge your fantasies, either. A little role-playing, a little voyeurism—whatever your fantasy, if you know your partner is into it, too—it can be a fun sexual excursion. Acting out your fantasies from time to time can be a healthy way to stretch your boundaries and explore each other. Just be conscious that overindulging in fantasy can sometimes take over—and then your mate can only get turned on if you wear heels and rub them all over his face. That's when fantasy becomes a fetish, that is, a sexual situation or an object that becomes absolutely necessary to sexual arousal. Too much fantasy play can make the fetish the ruler of your sexual kingdom, which is very limiting and sometimes downright boring. Just a heads up.

#62 ... Never have sex with a guy who keeps his socks on.

Picture a man who you think is so sexy, all revved up and ready to go, naked but for his socks. This is the epitome of *not* sexy. This is a man who can't *see* his socks because his, um, eagerness is in the way. This is a man who's not concerned with keeping up his end of the mystique and aura that help make sex so much fun. This is a man who just wants to jump you, which sometimes seems good enough, but you deserve a lot more!

Think of all the care and time and money you put into your appearance, thinking only of how sexy you want to be for him. Now think about how much the opposite of that a guy wearing his socks during sex is. It's just not right.

Your date doesn't need to be a metrosexual, preoccupied with his personal grooming and fine clothing. In fact, some of the sexiest guys are rough and tumble, with messy hair and five o'clock shadows and raggedy jeans. Whatever his type, though, he needs to know enough to take off his socks when he gets naked with you. Period.

Furthermore, his wearing socks can be a signal of where he's at emotionally. He keeps his socks on because he's not ready to bare all emotionally and they help him to feel secure and protected from you getting too close. Well, that's fine for him, but what makes him think you want those soft smelly things touching your legs?

I Can't Believe I Did That! I had been having a flirtation with a guy in my office for some time. I had gotten to where I was fantasizing about him all the time, definitely getting myself worked up for a possible fling. He had reached Adonis proportions in my imagination, which I guess is part of the fun of having a crush. One night, a bunch of us went out for drinks after work and this guy and I flirted madly all night, until he finally suggested we head to his apartment. I was *psyched*. We started groping and making out immediately, working our way to his bed as quick as we could get there. I could not have been hotter to have sex with this guy, and before I knew it we were having at it. How disappointed was I to look down and see this otherwise adorable naked guy on top of me, with his Gold Toe knee-length businessman socks still on his feet. That was a bucket of cold water thrown over my passion, believe me. And my crush on him was kaput.—Ali

If you encounter a guy who tries to keep his socks on during sex you can simply lay down the law: No socks or no sex. Or you can just get up and walk out. Because a guy who wants to wear socks during sex, especially if his excuse is that he's cold, is probably not going to light your Roman candle anyway.

Never have sex with a guy in socks UNLESS . . .

- He's wearing socks . . . and cowboy boots and tight jeans and T-shirt. There's nothing wrong with having sex with a hottie wearing *all* his clothes, including his socks.
- You're having sex in the Antarctic, outdoors in the middle of a snowstorm, in the meat freezer at the restaurant you both work at . . . you get the picture.
- He's an unbelievably attractive sock model.
- He's in desperate need of a pedi and is keeping them on for your safety.
- It's the middle of winter, your heat is out, and you get to keep yours on, too.

#63 ... Never be seduced by Mother Nature.

Despite what romance novels and popular magazines would have you believe, sex out in nature can be highly overrated. Those breathtaking photos in travel magazines that seduce you into a romantic getaway don't paint a complete picture of what sex might be like in these exotic locales. Mother Nature is not friendly to outdoor loving, especially the more you strip down. Beaches can make for rough sex, with those tiny grains of sand getting *everywhere*, which can totally dampen your desire. A literal roll in the hay—or a field—can make for scratchy, itchy, dusty sex. And while sex in the woods can turn you into a regular Adam and Eve, it can do too good of a job making you feel at one with nature as you encounter tree bark, crawling (and biting) bugs, dead leaves, broken branches, thorns, and critter droppings. Oh, and let's not forget about risks like coming away with poison ivy.

Jewel enjoyed a classic romp au naturel: "Once on a family vacation to St. Thomas, my boyfriend and I were desperate to find some privacy, away from my five siblings and parents. Naturally, we thought the beautiful white sand beach with its palm trees and lapping water would be perfect for making love. We snuck down late at night and stretched out under one of the palm trees. Very soon, we were, how shall I say, distracted by the scads of sand flies biting every little inch of our quite naked skin. Determined, we kept going until the final insult: a coconut literally bonked my boyfriend on the head. Even youthful lust couldn't overcome that blow and we gave up, scratching and itching all the way back to the condo. The lesson: tropical beaches are overrated as sex venues, or, sometimes there's trouble in paradise."

On the other hand, it's true that outdoor sex can offer a lot of variety and new sexual experiences. That in and of itself is thrilling and can be a lot of fun—and may make the occasional drawbacks well worth the adventure or discomfort. Doing it outdoors is especially appealing to those of us who have exhibitionist tendencies. Let's face it, being outdoors means you're wide open to exposure—and not only of the climatic kind. Sex with the risk of people stumbling upon you could be rousing. Imagine sailing to the far side of a lake, stretching out on

I Can't Believe I Did That!   My boyfriend and I were new in our relationship—the time when you can't keep your hands off each other. We were walking through the grounds of a local university one summer night, when we just decided to do it on a picnic table. Things were going fine, until we heard an entire crowd around us—the girls' summer soccer camp had just returned to their dorm! We zipped up and dashed out of there, but not before realizing that both his knees and the small of my back were embedded with splinters. Talk about postcoital bliss.—Sherry

a warm flat granite boulder, and "hoping" no one catches the two of you . . . you get the idea.

If you're going to take to the great outdoors with some intimate activity in mind, make sure you have a blanket or towel. Bug repellent is a must. Maintain a sense of humor. Be ready for anything. And, most important, have an alternative to your plan—should you and your lover get caught up in a thunderstorm, hear the cry of a lone wolf, get bit on the butt by a sand crab, or encounter an unfriendly skunk, you'll know what to do.

#64 ... Never ask your boyfriend which of your friends he would sleep with if he weren't with you.

You can take a perfectly happy relationship and completely turn it upside down with that one simple question. You just don't need to know which of your friends he would shag if he wasn't getting hot and heavy with you. A smart man would carefully refuse to answer. But even a smart man can get worn down by your badgering him for an answer—and once you've forced a name out of him, he'll never stop paying for this mistake. You will never be able to get it out of your mind and you'll never think about him or your friend the same way again. You will begin to see her as competition and you will begin to see him as untrustworthy—even though neither of them has done a thing to deserve the distinction. You will obsess over what he likes about her, what she's got that you haven't, whether she's attracted to him, whether they'd get together if given the opportunity.

Posing the who-would-you-sleep-with question, even if it's just out of harmless curiosity, will bring out insecurities you never knew you had and will turn you into a complete head case, as Rhoda reveals: "I made the mistake of asking my man who he'd want of my friends. What made it hard to swallow was that it wasn't the hottest one, whom I expected him to pick. It was the one I would've least expected, which made me wonder, what made her so special? Then I drove myself crazy obsessing over whether or not he'd ever try to do her on the sly. I ended up needing to break off my friendship with her because I couldn't take her being around my boyfriend anymore."

Rhoda's story is a sad one in that she lost a friend over this silly but loaded question. It's even more tragic that the friend never even knew that she simply got picked out of the lineup by the boyfriend and that's the only reason the friendship came to an end.

But if genuinely curious about the kinds of ladies your beau finds attractive, stick with territory that's a tad safer. Ask him which Hollywood stars or popular singers he thinks are hot—what guy doesn't lust after Shakira, for example, and how much of a threat could she possibly be to you? She's practically a fantasy, for heaven's sake! Or, play a game of either/or. Make him choose between two famous hotties: Marilyn Monroe or Rita Hayworth. Betty or Veronica. Britney or Christina. *That* can be a fun conversation.

No matter what kind of pointlessly probing question you ask in this vein, be prepared to have the cards turned on you. Your lover may want to know who else *you* find attractive. All's fair in love and war and in this case, you should expect that he may not like what he hears, either.

#65 ... Never give road head in a moving vehicle.

Fooling around while driving is an age-old form of entertainment, and road head is certainly on the top ten list of risky, risqué fun to be had in this vein. Oh, the thrill of it! But, having to explain to the police or your parents that you and your lover got into a car accident one dark and stormy night because of road head is why this is *so* never. And that's not even considering a worst-case scenario of injury or death. Just think of the headlines: "Couple Die from Careless Car Sex."

So if you're all sexually charged, save yourself a big headache, as well as other body aches, by adhering to this oral pleasuring road rule: Pull over. (Although, see Never #11.)

To be completely safe for yourself and other motorists, pull off the road and by all means have at it. No matter what anyone tells you, it counts as road head if it happens in a car. Purists,

I Can't Believe I Did That! When my boyfriend Justin and I took a cross-country trip, I'd go down on him every few days to break the monotony of long drives. Part of the thrill was that while we'd be speeding down the highway, he would accelerate as he got more turned on, which was more of a turn-on for me. We were both totally getting into it until, with his attention elsewhere, he hit a pothole in the middle of the interstate. As his unit was forced into the back of my throat and my teeth made contact, I heard him yelp in pain. I couldn't help but bite down with the impact—it was horrible. Between my sore tonsils and his swollen member, neither of us felt like much action for the rest of the week. We also decided to set up road rules for such future play.—Beth

you can keep the motor running if it makes you feel better, though the guilt of adding to the Ozone later can kill your O. And if you must stay on the road, at least stick with some hand action, which won't put you both in as vulnerable a position should he lose control with his climax.

#66 ... Never have sex during a rebound.

When you've been hurt, dumped, or find yourself missing a lover who has newly become your ex, having rebound sex is one of the worst things you can do to yourself. When on the rebound, one is often in a vulnerable state of mind, longing for a self-esteem boost or comfort or attention or being made to feel desirable—or, ultimately, your ex. And any of those emotional needs can make you do something you may not truly want to do with somebody you really don't want to be intimate with. You can end up feeling empty, unfulfilled, or upset with yourself for having given yourself away so soon after your last love affair. Even worse, longing for everything you just lost, it can be all too easy to hope for it all over again with your rebound, only to be let down again—a pain doubled.

Furthermore, you can end up hurting the person you're rebounding with if you don't want more than a one-night stand or fling. As Pierre shares, "I met this stunning woman weeks after she had lost her husband. She was understandably devastated and I tried to be a source of comfort with her. We slept together, but it never went any further than that. To this day, I'm still taken by her and have to wonder if we might be together now had we not been intimate so soon. She really wasn't ready for it, even though she thought it would help her deal with her loss."

While a few can handle rebound sex with no guilt, no qualms, no confusion, most cannot. Make sure you take care of yourself during this period. This doesn't mean that you should hibernate and shun the world of intimacy. Be close to other people who are important to you. Hang out with your friends or family. Attend a yoga class or exercise. Go on a casual date. But don't force yourself to be in a place you're not ready to be, whether it's being sexually active again or diving headfirst into another relationship. You need to give yourself the time to heal and process what you've felt and learned. Once you're in a better place, sex can be just the ticket. It can help you close the door on the past, reminding you that there are others out there. It can be restorative to be physically close to someone else, and sex can chemically and emotionally boost your mood. Just give yourself a healing break first. Then you'll be able to have exactly the kind of sex and/or relationship you're really ready to enjoy.

#67 ... Never go home with someone else just to make your guy jealous.

"My bachelorette party was on the same night as my fiancé's bachelor party. The plan was for everyone to get absolutely piss drunk and then for the two groups to meet up. When all of us found ourselves finally closing down the last bar, I wasn't finding any humor in the hilarious stories the guys had about the strippers who had been all over my fiancé. To get back at him, I started hopelessly flirting with the blue-eyed babe tending bar and eventually had so much to drink that I was about to go home with him. Needless to say, my fiancé wasn't too happy with me and was annoyed that I was trying to make him jealous. We kissed and made up though, and thought nothing more of it until the night of our wedding reception. Guess who was DJing the party? It put a dark cloud over what should've been a happy evening for us."

Sabrina's story, while a bit of a coincidence, demonstrates one of the ways that provoking jealousy can come back to bite you. But there are many other ways, too, most of them relationship threatening.

Purposely doing something—including hooking up with someone else—to get your guy jealous is a bad path to follow. Here's why: Provoking someone to jealousy as a way to "test" his feelings for you is really just a test of his capacity for jealousy, *not* an accurate measure of his feelings.

There's nothing about jealousy that's good for a relationship. When you set out to make him jealous, you only see what jealousy looks like on him—harsh, hurt, angry, unpredictable, or even violent—not the depth of his feeling for you. It's a Pandora's Box you're opening, as these feelings are extremely difficult to put away once they've come to the surface. If you've made him jealous, he won't look at you and think, "Oh, how much I love her"; instead, he'll feel threatened and possessive and think something more like, "Can I trust her?"

The volatile state of mind that jealousy puts him in can overtake his feelings for you. That is, it can confuse him to the point of not being able to distinguish his jealousy over you from his feelings for you. And wouldn't you rather know how much he loves you than how crazy-maniac with jealousy he can be? One is nice and clear and grounded. The other is just, well, crazy!

Finally, you may as well forget the relationship if you try to make him jealous by flirting or hooking up with his best friend (or worst enemy), or his boss, or someone else he knows well. On the surface, he may be able to "get over it" after you wake up and quit doing it. But he'll *never* stop seething and stewing over it and feeling deeply hurt and betrayed by you. So if you want to continue to grow your relationship with this guy, don't poison it by needlessly provoking his jealousy.

Never make him jealous UNLESS . . .

- You don't want to be with your guy anymore and you want to give him a reason to give you the boot.
- Your relationship is on life support and you want to give it shock therapy to see if there's anything left to it.

#68 ... Never lie about having an STD.

Think about the last time you had the flu. Amidst your body shakes, fever, sweats, vomiting, and diarrhea, chances are you were not only wondering where you picked up this bug, but cursing the person who randomly gave it to you, too. All it takes is one person who doesn't feel well, but goes to work or school sick anyway, to share a bug that can knock you off your feet for a week. How inconsiderate! If you'd only known this person was sick, you could have avoided contact with him or protected yourself from infection by washing your hands or wearing a mask—or simply staying *away*.

Now what if that inconsiderate person was prancing around with a sexually transmitted disease and having wanton, unprotected sex and not telling partners? It's criminally inconsiderate. In fact, a court in California recently ruled that people need to tell their partners about their status.

When you're infected with a sexually transmitted disease (STD)—more recently called a "sexually transmitted infection"—the only ethical thing to do is to tell your potential partner so he can make his own decision about whether to risk acquiring this infection. In being honest about your STD status, you're showing respect for your partner and your partner's health, as well as confidence in your ability to deal with it yourself. You're taking care of your partner, the relationship,

I Can't Believe I Did That!   I had been having a recurrent yeast infection problem, but I didn't know enough about it to know why it kept coming back. I had used over-the-counter meds time and time again, but nothing seemed to help. I was sleeping with this guy at the time and I was too embarrassed to tell him about the infection for fear he'd think I was gross and not want to be with me. He even asked me once why there was white stuff on his penis when he pulled out and I played dumb, saying all girls are like that sometimes. It wasn't until I finally went in to see my OB/GYN for an oral medication that I learned that in not telling my guy and in not getting him treated too, I was reinfecting myself every time I had sex with him! I also found out that yeast infections are considered sexually transmitted diseases because they can be passed during sex. The worst thing, though, was that I didn't have a chance to tell him before he went to his doctor, only to find out that he had a throat infection from having gone down on me. Yuck!—Alex and your own body, including avoiding the chance of reinfecting yourself.

Get medical treatment for your infection and abstain from sex play until you have a clean bill of health. Putting your own or someone else's health at risk is *never* worth a quickie. Your partner should be grateful and respect the fact that you had the courage to share your status with him. And if he's not—if he reacts with judgment or makes you feel stigmatized—throw him back. That just shows that he's not worth keeping.

#69 ... Never say the wrong name during sex.

Screaming, shouting, moaning, or gasping a name other than your lover's during sex never turns out well. While many people fantasize about other people (even past lovers) when they're having sex, almost nobody wants to actually know that you're lost in a fantasy of someone other than present company, especially when you're climaxing. It's the ultimate show-stopper, libido-killer, and big dis. Unless your lover is into that person too, chances are it's not going to be well received. You'll have a hurt soul and bruised ego to deal with, often without good explanation. *It just happened; it just slipped out. Nothing was meant by it.* You *made me come, really.*

While those may be valid excuses and reassurances, they're not always going to be good ones. So be ready for some serious ego smoothing, and then take a time-out with yourself to make sure that shouting out so-and-so's name really didn't hold any significance. If you aren't convinced yourself, how can you expect your partner to be? It may be an indication that you need to reconsider your relationship. A lover may be willing to put up with this kind of insult once; very few would be willing to take it twice.

If you're the type who gets lost in the moment and the wrong-name syndrome is familiar, try another tack—stick to "God." *Oh, God! Oh, God!* What guy doesn't think of that as the ultimate compliment?

#70 ... Never say never.

We live in a world of nevers—too many, in fact. So it's important to remember that nevers don't always have to be adhered to in the strictest sense. If we listened to and heeded all of the nevers we're told daily, surely life would be dull. When would we have any adventures? What good stories would we have to tell? Where would juicy gossip about others gone wrong come from?

Nevers are nevers for a reason. But there's also something to be said about living, growing, and learning by experiencing some nevers you probably shouldn't have done. Many situations are not as clear-cut and easily addressed with a never, and sometimes you have to use your judgment and figure out what to do. Nevers are there to merely guide us. Sometimes we need to take a chance, even if the outcome isn't what we expected or hoped for. Sometimes we want to push the envelope and find out what all the fuss is about. Sometimes we need to commit a never to get to a better place with ourselves and to be able to handle bigger challenges.

Some of your greatest life experiences and lessons can come from doing what comes naturally to you and seeing where it takes you, even if it involves these tricky nevers. People may surprise you; the gods may bless you. There's risk with nearly everything in life and, with a mix of smarts, luck, and good energy, there can be a bit of a payoff when you choose to forgo a never's wise warning. Think of all the great things that have been accomplished because people didn't listen to naysayers and nevers. So if you need to discover and explore, take a chance, put yourself out there, live a little, and—for better or worse—never say never.

Acknowledgments

Perhaps one of the best things about being a writer is being able to publicly thank all of the special people who make things happen behind the scenes. Many thanks go out to . . .

The amazing ladies at Lark Productions—Lisa DiMona, Karen Watts, and Robin Dellabough—for their time, energy, and contributions to this project.

My lovely, talented editor and friend at Adams Media, Jennifer Kushnier, for all of her efforts and feedback, and for having the faith in me to tackle this project.

Everyone at Adams Media, especially Beth Gissinger-Rivera and Karen Cooper, for their hard work.

My parents, Charles G. Fulbright and Ósk Lárusdóttir Fulbright, for all of their generous support.

All of my friends, especially Bianca Angelino Grimaldi and Tiffany J. Franklin, for their ideas and tireless cheerleading efforts.

The many people, who cannot be named, who entrusted me with stories to help other people both laugh and learn from their nevers.

About the Author

Originally from Iceland, sexologist, author, relationship expert, and columnist Yvonne K. Fulbright holds a master's degree in human sexuality from the University of Pennsylvania and is currently finishing her PhD in International Community Health, with a sexual health focus, at New York University. She is a member of the American Association of Sex Educators, Counselors, and Therapists and the Society for the Scientific Study of Sexuality. She is the author of two previous books, *The Hot Guide to Safer Sex* and *Touch Me There! A Hands-On Guide to Your Orgasmic Hot Spots.* To learn more about Yvonne and her work, visit *www.sexualitysource.com.*